What they are saying about
Extreme Competition

As one of the nation's most-respected and best-performing telecommunications companies, Cincinnati Bell competes in an unpredictable and turbulent marketplace. In order to beat the competition, we must first compete against ourselves. We are committed to a "defend and grow" strategy, and use bundling to engage in both defensive and offensive plays. In short, we have no choice but to be the extreme competitor described in Peter's intriguing book, nor do you.
John F. Cassidy, President and CEO, Cincinnati Bell

Companies in Asia and Eastern Europe are creating new and dramatically different offerings, stealing market share, and rendering many incumbent companies obsolete. *Extreme Competition* eloquently describes how companies must rethink their business strategies, from the ground up, to respond to the realities of 21st century competition.
Bryan Maizlish, CTO, Program Team, Lockheed Martin IS&S, and coauthor of *IT Portfolio Management Step by Step*

Peter Fingar sounds a piercing wake-up call to business leaders. He makes it clear that to survive it's essential to develop an obsessive, even paranoid, attention to business processes, and to manage them for continuous and unrelenting innovation. Readers and companies that have low adversity quotients on this issue will become history, extremely fast.
Kiran Garimella, CIO, GE Healthcare Financial Services

Peter Fingar draws an exciting portrait of what lies ahead as globalization and technological innovation magnify both the opportunity and competition at hand. A must read for all businesses looking to navigate this new world paradigm.
Joseph Halpern, Partner, Halpern Capital

The world's economies are going through a period of great transition, and in many industries, the rules are changing before our very eyes. Today, companies must ask how an ever more connected world will change the rules in their industries. *Extreme Competition* offers the in-depth analysis needed to formulate those questions, and chart a path ahead.
Edward C. Grady, CEO, Brooks Automation

Companies that have embraced Fingar's message are moving ahead, and creating innovative new business models so remarkable that in some instances they appear to give away their core products and services. How can they do that? *Extreme Competition* captures the moment and provides the answer.
Steve Towers, CEO, Business Process Management Group, Warwick, England

Reading Fingar's book on the plane made up for the hockey game I missed watching. The book's pace was faster and the impact made me feel like I was on the ice getting hit. And unlike a game that is forgotten when it is over, the ideas and challenges presented in this book simply cannot be forgotten.
Dave Hollander, Co-inventor of XML, the Lingua Franca of the Internet

Leading companies employ what we at AMR Research call *Predatory Supply Chains*. They utilize their supply chain superiority to become fierce competitors to rule their markets. They deliver 20% more perfect orders, hold a third less inventory, and have lower costs equal to 5% of revenue. This book defines the new rules of the game.
Eric Austvold, Research Director, AMR Research

By the author of the landmark books

BUSINESS PROCESS MANAGEMENT:
THE THIRD WAVE

IT DOESN'T MATTER:
BUSINESS PROCESSES DO

THE REAL-TIME ENTERPRISE:
COMPETING ON TIME

THE DEATH OF 'E' AND
THE BIRTH OF THE REAL NEW ECONOMY

Acclaim for our books:
Featured book recommendation
Harvard Business School's *Working Knowledge*

Book of the Year
Internet World

www.mkpress.com

Extreme Competition

Innovation and the
Great 21st Century Business Reformation

Peter Fingar

With coverage of the global business hot spots
by the following contributors:
Sandeep Arora (Bangalore, India)
Sue Bushell (Sydney, Australia)
Hitoshi Shirai (Tokyo, Japan)
Abhinandhan Prateek (Hyderabad, India)
Mark McGregor (London, England)
Omar Mark Ragel (Saudi Arabia and Bahrain)
Frits Bussemaker (Amsterdam, The Netherlands)
Steve Towers (Warwick, United Kingdom)
Shridhar Rangarajan (Pune, India)
Jesse Shiah (Taipei, Republic of China)
Gene Weng (Shanghai, People's Republic of China)
Charles Koh (Seoul, South Korea)
Chee-Seng Low (Singapore, Republic of Singapore)
Jae-Hyoung Yoo (Seoul, South Korea)

Meghan-Kiffer Press
Tampa, Florida, USA
www.mkpress.com
Innovation at the Intersection of Business and Technology

Publisher's Cataloging-in-Publication Data

Fingar, Peter.
Extreme Competition: Innovation and the Great 21st Century Business Reformation
/ Peter Fingar, - 1st ed.
p. cm.
    Includes appendix.
    ISBN-10: 0-929652-38-X   ISBN-13: 978-0929652-38-2
    1. Management 2. Technological innovation. 3. Diffusion of innovations.
    4. Globalization—Economic aspects. 5. Information technology. 6. Information Society. 7. Organizational change. I. Fingar, Peter. II. Title

HM48.F75 2006   2005936864
303.48'33–dc22   CIP

Published by Meghan-Kiffer Press
310 East Fern Street — Suite G
Tampa, FL 33604 USA

Company and product names mentioned herein are the trademarks or registered trademarks of their respective owners.

Meghan-Kiffer books are available at special quantity discounts for corporate education and training use. For more information write Special Sales, Meghan-Kiffer Press, Suite G, 310 East Fern Street, Tampa, Florida 33604 or email sales@mkpress.com

Meghan-Kiffer Press
USA

Printed in the United States of America. SAN 249-7980
MK Printing 10 9 8 7 6 5 4 3 2 1

*This book is dedicated to extreme competitors,
who many may wish to burn at the stake.*

*Although mainstream economic thought holds that America's history
of creativity and entrepreneurialism will allow it to adapt to the rise of such
emerging economies as India and China, I think that is so much wishful
thinking. Globalization will not only finish off what's left of American
manufacturing, but will turn so-called knowledge workers, which were supposed to be America's competitive advantage, into just another global
commodity. I'm really concerned about the growing disrespect for science in
America.*
—Andy Grove, Co-Founder, Intel.

*America's working middle class has been eroding for a generation, and
it may be about to wash away completely. Something must be done.*
—Paul Krugman, *The New York Times.*

*Thousands of years ago, the first man discovered how to make fire. He
was probably burned at the stake he had taught his brothers to light. He
was considered an evildoer who had dealt with a demon mankind dreaded.
But thereafter men had fire to keep them warm, to cook their food, to light
their caves. He had left them a gift they had not conceived and he had lifted
darkness off the earth. Centuries later, the first man invented the wheel.
He was probably torn on the rack he had taught his brothers to build. He
was considered a transgressor who ventured into forbidden territory. But
thereafter, men could travel past any horizon. He had left them a gift they
had not conceived and he had opened the roads of the world.*
—*The Fountainhead.*

Foreword by Rajesh Jain

Today's world looks very different from the vantage point of where I reside here in Mumbai, India. It is a world full of infinite opportunities as companies seek to leapfrog the legacy of decades of slow development. It is a world with youthful energy and money being unleashed as one navigates the new malls and restaurants coming up all over. It is a world where mobile phones connect people who never used a landline before—and perhaps will never use a desktop computer, opting for more advanced NetPCs and wireless devices of all manner.

It is also a world where the services juggernaut in urban India is complemented by the largely agricultural rural economy, where hundreds of millions still live in poverty. It's a world where the old still exists and, at times, even dominates the new. The contrasts may be stark, but there is one thing that is ubiquitous in my homeland: Optimism! For the first time in living memory, there is a belief that tomorrow will be better than today. That perception alone can make all the difference. I see not just the Old India of yesterday, but the New India of tomorrow. It is an India that will be built in a world of extreme competition, and extreme opportunities—powered by transformations and disruptions.

Disruptions are technological shifts that can provide opportunities for newcomers to take on incumbents—and perhaps usurp their power. It happens all the time. Today's king is not guaranteed to be tomorrow's emperor. We have seen this in history and politics, and we also see it in business. While at times, incumbents hasten their downfall by questionable decisions (in retrospect), at other times entrepreneurial start-ups, with some luck, race their way to the top. While there is no magic formula, understanding disruptions and key trends is crucial for success. This is the journey Peter takes us through—from business process transformation creating real-time enterprises, to the combined buying power of the billions in the world's emerging, underserved markets. Today's world is one of complexity, but a thorough understanding of the underlying principles can help in reaching new markets and customers.

I am a strong believer that there is a tectonic shift taking place in the world. The East is rising. And with a reverse brain drain of talent taking place from the West, innovations are now starting to flow from the world's emerging markets—with the potential to blowback to the developed nations. Today's non-consumers are becoming the new battleground—because their delight will shed light on the economic future of all nations. What is needed is an understanding of the present to build a vision of the future. *Extreme Competition* provides the needed framework to peer through the fog of today, and unravel the contours of tomorrow.

Rajesh Jain, Managing Director of Netcore, and Founder of IndiaWorld, Mumbai, India

Foreword by Tom McCarty

Like the proverbial frog in the boiling pot of water, business leaders may find themselves in such a sea of complex, external forces that they are slowly "boiling to death," frozen in their current state, unable to make the leap to the next business model. In this book, Peter Fingar issues a wake up call to those leaders that may still be thinking that "this too shall pass." He provides a compelling summary of the major forces that are shaping our current environment.

Having led the Six Sigma for Suppliers initiative at Motorola University, where Six Sigma was born, and as a Blackbelt who has been working with business leaders to create competitive advantage through business process management practices, I am especially encouraged by Peter's insights into the importance of process excellence as a path to success in the future. Of particular interest to me is the focus on processes that extend across the value chain, tying supply and production seamlessly through to full delivery of customer benefits.

Leaders that are able to re-think their business processes in ways that remove traditional boundaries between supply processes, production processes and customer processes, can achieve extreme competitive advantage in reaching global markets and delivering customer benefits at previously unimagined rates of speed and efficiency. "Grok process!" will be the new battle cry for leaders that embrace Peter Fingar's thoughtful advice. I view this book as a must read for those leaders.

Tom McCarty, Executive Vice President and Six Sigma Practice Leader, Jones Lang LaSalle, and former Vice President of Consulting and Training Services at Motorola University.

Preface

Ideas are easy; books are hard. As a business practitioner and manager for almost 40 years, with a few stints as a professor of computing studies, I have been working at the intersection of business and technology for a long time. Along the way I've sometimes been engrossed in innovation; and at other times, engrossed in the boredom of "yet another computer system conversion." I've spent quality time at the home of John Vincent Atanasoff, the man who invented the electronic digital computer. I've enjoyed amazing stories from my daughter-in-law's great uncle, John Cocke, the father of RISC architecture that powers today's mighty Macintosh computers. Cocke won the Turing Award, the equivalent of a Nobel prize in computer science. I've worked with pioneers in artificial intelligence, with the coinventor of XML, the lingua franca of the Internet, and I commuted to Cairo, Egypt to work on one of the biggest Internet projects ever envisioned. I first used the Internet in 1969, before it was called the Internet, while on my first job out of college at GTE Data Services. GTEDS was striving to become a computer utility, a kind of computing which IBM and others now call "On Demand."

In short, when it comes to the intersection of business and technology, I've kind of been there, done that. Little amazes me, and over the years I've been impatient with the slow assimilation of technology and the lack of impact it should have already made. Every time my PC hangs, I scream, does anybody in Redmond know what year it is? Why am I putting up with this crap in 2005?

But, you know what? I feel like an awed 18-year old again

when it comes to what's happening at the intersection of business and technology today. It wasn't the invention of the computer that triggered a great 21st century transformation, it was Sputnik in 1957, and the beginning of global telecommunications. Now all the world's computers are linked by the Net, shrinking the planet to the size of the screen on your cell phone. The last 40 years have been a kind of warm up to the real thing. The great dot-com crash of 2000 wasn't the signal for the beginning of the end, it was a signal that we had reached the end of the beginning. The tinkering phase of the Internet was complete, and now it's time to get on with the real transformation of business and society.

Clyde Prestowitz, author and former counselor to the Secretary of Commerce in the Reagan Administration, shocks us with his revelations that three billion new capitalists have entered the work force, triggering the great shift of wealth and power to the East—which means all is changed, utterly.

To distill this great 21st century business transformation and what it portends for businesses and individuals, I decided to open up the screen on my desktop and reached out to experts from India, China, Europe, Japan, Australia, Korea, Singapore and the Mid-East to bring up-to-the minute research to these pages. Those experts brought fresh information you'd only hear around the water cooler in high-tech organizations in Shanghai, London, Bangalore, Taipei, Tokyo, Hyderabad, Sydney, Riyadh, Manama, Seoul and Singapore—stepping up to the plate (their computer screens) to make this synthesis and distillation reflect a global snapshot of the new world of extreme competition. Although we were continents apart during the development of this book, we were virtual office mates through our many collaborations using the Net and Skype Internet telephone, messaging and file sharing (total cost of collaborating this way? $Zero). Such intimate interaction with individual knowledge workers, scattered around the globe, wasn't possible before the world was wired, and gives you a hint of what this book is about—extreme collaboration without borders.

Through the stories of innovation and transformation that appear in this book, our hope is that you benefit from what we have summarized about the new rules of the global economy. To that end, I've included Extreme Readings for further study so you can discover that something very old (this thing we call business) is new again. We hope that this condensed treatment of a huge subject will stimulate you to learn more, much more, as you strive to win at the game of extreme competition, as businesses, and as individuals.

My very best wishes for your continued success,

Peter Fingar
Tampa, Florida, USA

Contents

Are You Ready for Extreme Competition?

"The dogmas of the quiet past are inadequate to the stormy present. The occasion is piled high with difficulty and we must rise with the occasion. As our case is new we must think anew and act anew."
—Abraham Lincoln.

There are some fierce new competitors on the block, ready to engage you and your company in extreme competition. They've reformed 20th century business doctrines, ideologies and practices with 21st century thinking. They play hardball and dominate their industries. Through their laser-focused scopes, they have their eyes on you and your company. Your customers are their target, and they'd do almost anything to take them away from you.

Indeed, there is a next big thing in business, but it's not about dot-com booms; it's about operational innovation and business transformation, driven by the emergence of a wired world.

Are you ready to engage in extreme competition? Do you have a complete understanding of the five forces driving the global business transformation? Has your company addressed the sixteen new realities of extreme business? Do you have the thirteen strategies for extreme competition in place?

These are not high-level academic questions for economists, they are questions that your company and you, personally, must answer. Further, one-time answers are not enough, for as with any structural change of this scope, it's not obvious in the beginning how the great 21st century business reformation will be played out. As events unfold, these questions will be asked over and over by companies and individuals that want to win in the decade ahead.

With insights from leading business practitioners across the globe, this book sets forth a framework for understanding the structural transformation underway, explains the unstoppable five drivers of change, describes the sixteen new realities of business, and explores thirteen useful patterns for formulating business strategy. Together these analyses will help answer *the* business question of our time, "Are you ready for extreme competition?"

The Great 21st Century Business Reformation.

Technology has a history of wresting power from complacent elites and forcibly redistributing it in ways that rock the foundations of the known world. What mankind gained from Johannes Gutenberg's invention of the printing press, circa 1450, is incalculable. But for one, it led to the tearing apart of information power held by the church and courts. The Gutenberg press, in putting the Bible into the hands of the common man, helped weaken the grip of the venal priests of the 15th century Church of England and paved the way for the geopolitical earthquake that was Martin Luther's *Reformation*. It was indeed the invention of the printing press and the 1455 publication of the Gutenberg Bible that *enabled* Luther's Reformation, which began on Oct. 31, 1517, when he nailed his 95 Theses to the church door in Wittenberg, Germany. When summoned to appear before the Emperor to answer for his writings; Luther gave his timeless reply: "I cannot submit my faith either to the Pope or to the Councils, because it is clear as day they have frequently erred and contradicted each other. Unless therefore, I am convinced by the testimony of Scripture . . . I cannot and will not retract . . . Here I stand, I can do no other. So help me God, Amen." With the availability of the Bible to everyone, the power of the church hierarchy to interpret, filter and control information vanished. What followed is, of course, history.

Now the Internet, in seizing business information from the corporations who have hoarded it, and putting it in the hands of the common customer, is precipitating an economic power shift from the Atlantic to the Pacific. Companies will never be the same. With the tectonic plates heaving under our feet, we're entering the era of the great 21st century business *reformation*, and corporations had better start swimming or expect to sink like a stone in a tsunami. What mankind gained from Tim Berners Lee's invention of the World Wide Web, circa 1991, is incalculable. But for one, it's leading to the tearing apart of information power held by bureaucracies in the huge corporations born of the Industrial Age. With the availability of the Web to virtually everyone, the power of the management hierarchy to interpret, filter and control information vanished. What followed is, of course, making history, and powering the great 21st century business reformation. Without actually saying these words, Amazon's Jeff Bezos could easily have said: "I cannot submit my faith either to the incumbent retailers or to their tightly-held supply chains, because it is clear as day they have frequently erred and contradicted each other. Unless therefore, I am convinced by the testimony of the Web . . . I cannot and will not retract . . . Here I stand, I can do no other. So help me God, Amen."

With the universal connectivity of the Internet, all is changed, changed utterly. It has to do with bewildering new possibilities related to business processes, the way work gets done, by whom and for whom.

It's like the creation of a new primordial process soup,

from which new forms of supply chains, known as value webs, are bubbling up across the globe.

A company used to physically cluster its employees to foster information exchange. To achieve proximity, skyscrapers were built to house information workers. Middle management was the information conduit and filter, with "need to know" being the guiding principle for information dissemination up and down the chain of command. Communication proceeded top-down, through a well-managed hierarchy, replete with fiefdoms of information control. Information flowing upward was filtered through layers of bureaucrats. Strategy was encumbered by this structure, and change of direction was comparable in difficulty to that of turning an aircraft carrier on a dime. Forecasts were the basis for planning, but by their very definition, forecasts are wrong.

Years ago, Dr. Michael Porter, Harvard Business School's authority on competition and strategy, concluded that, "Activities, then, are the basics of competitive advantage. Overall advantage or disadvantage results from all a company's activities. The essence of strategy is choosing to perform activities differently than rivals do." But it's not so easy to change the activities a company currently performs, even if these are now dysfunctional work patterns, for ingrained work habits are hard to break. Even with the universal connectivity of the Internet, many companies still operate in the same basic ways they have always operated—coordinating work manually, conducting meetings, shuffling paper and making repeated phone calls to correct even the simplest of errors in day-to-day business transactions.

Meanwhile, others, some of which are highlighted in this book, actually conduct business with real-time business processes that reach across the globe using the Internet. Using the principles of business process management, they have made deep structural changes in their organizations that make them different. They are *time-based competitors* and are swift to make major course corrections, while delighting their customers day in and day out with *responsiveness*, rolling out innovations with regularity. It's all in how they do what they do, and they clearly have reinvented how they do what they do.

21st century "operational transformation" requires looking outside the walls of a given company and managing the complete value-delivery system, from its customers' customers, to its suppliers' suppliers. While the Internet provides the digital nervous system for the 21st century company, a new generation of business interaction software is emerging that provides what's needed to harness the universal connectivity of the Internet for business advantage.

Extreme Competition

There is no real precedent for today's rush to the globalization of white-collar work, and the growing power of transnational corporations (GE, Citigroup, and ExxonMobil) that have come to dominate the business world and are beyond the control of any government—in fact, their lobbies are so powerful that they are often said to control governments.

But these and other lesser known rising stars in the global economy aren't just about largeness, they are about the fusion of business operations and information technology that connects every person and every machine across a global business ecosystem. In an endless pursuit of innovation, companies of thousands of employees, and sole proprietors alike, strive to distinguish themselves, and avoid commoditization so they can demand a premium for their goods and services.

The days of market stability and competitive advantage

from a single innovation are over. Today, companies must respond to new entrants in their industries that come from nowhere. And they must not just innovate, they must set the *pace of innovation,* gaining temporary advantage, one innovation at a time, and then move on to the next.

These new realities call for a new approach to management, and new capabilities to execute on innovation in an increasingly wired and global marketplace. The ability not only to sense and respond to market change, but to also anticipate customer needs, and shape markets, will become the core competencies for successful companies, large and small.

As companies try to come to grips with the new realities of 21st century business competition, they often turn their attention to Joseph Schumpeter's ideas of "creative destruction"[1] as the engine of the renovation, and technology's role as the agent of change. As we are dragged kicking and screaming into the 21st century, we will no doubt witness the emergence of a post-industrial form of company with new structures, ideas, operating fundamentals and challenges— along with a replacement of much 20th century business gospel. The doctrines, dogmas and practices of 20th century business operations are being questioned by a fierce new breed of competitor that, described in terms used by legendary football coach, Jake Gaither, is "agile, mobile and [often] hostile."

Remember when Sears was the 800-pound gorilla in retailing? Remember Delta as the most admired airline? Remember when you ordered "Good to the last drop" Maxwell House coffee at a restaurant? Remember when you wanted to buy a new car, you checked out all three car makers? Remember, a few decades ago, when globalization was about sending blue-collar work overseas and you thought that was the end of using this term in political debates?

There is no doubt something new is going on in business, though it may not be clear exactly what.

The new breed of 21st century business competitor has fused its business operations and technology to the point of unity, where the technology and the business leaders of winning companies are no longer at loggerheads, they feed off each other.

This new breed of companies uses the Internet as a digital nervous system to make deep structural changes in their core business processes.

They innovate not just with clever new products, they innovate with the services wrapped around those products: OnStar, originally developed from the work of Blue Octane, an IBM ExtremeBlue internship team, allows General Motors to sell you, not just a car, but an ongoing service that provides "peace of mind on the road."

They innovate by how they operate, how they deliver their *services,* how they *do* what they do, the ways they conduct their business operations at the delight of their customers. They go beyond just delivering products or services, and, as Starbucks taught us, on to delivering *experiences* that command a premium, and even change lifestyles.

They go to the ends of the earth to employ $.09 an hour factory workers and $20,000 per year PhDs in science and technology.

They disrupt their industries by weaving a tapestry of business processes with trading partners that allow them to offer unprecedented convenience and affordability to their customers, especially those who were *nonconsumers* before a game-changing innovation was introduced. For the pioneering Indian company, Novatium, with its slogan, "computing for the next billion," the market for affordable computing for the masses ($100 PCs) in countries like Brazil, China, India, Russia, and the working poor in developed countries is the computing world's next frontier and biggest pot of gold.

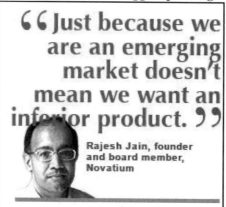

❝ Just because we are an emerging market doesn't mean we want an inferior product. ❞

Rajesh Jain, founder and board member, Novatium

They seek University of Michigan business expert, C.K. Prahalad's fortune at the bottom of the pyramid. Prahalad is author of *The Fortune at the Bottom of the Pyramid: Eradicating Poverty Through Profits*. While most companies continue to focus on the wealthy Western markets for selling their goods and services, India's Tata Group is building the $2,200 car. From the $100 PC to the $2,200 car, innovations that allow companies to make a profit in underserved markets will no doubt find their way to even the wealthiest nations. Companies that miss this trend will not only miss out on the emerging markets in Asia, the Middle East, Africa, and Latin America, they will come to find fierce new competitors landing on their shores and wreaking havoc in established markets (call it *blowback* if you like), regardless of a country's wealth. Necessity truly is the mother of innovation.

They spin a digital information web that can pick up on far away demand signals, sensing and responding to the slightest of vibrations from activity on the Web (technically called complex event processing). They use real-time information, generated both within the firm and across the value-delivery system, to trigger custom business processes to get work done over the Web—for their customers, employees, suppliers, and trading partners.

Their call center volumes decline as their customers and business partners solve their own issues by tapping a digital *concierge* who serves up process-powered self-service, gaining double leverage by slashing customer care costs, while delighting customers with a whole new experience of self-reliance.

They make-to-demand rather than make-to-forecast, and demand signals drive not only their flexible manufacturing, but also their flexible R&D portfolios.

They represent a "neo-merchant class," on a course with the Dutch Golden Age of long ago. As noted in Wikipedia.org, "A merchant class characterizes many pre-modern societies. Its status can range from high (even achieving titles like that of merchant prince or nabob) to low, such as in Chinese culture, due to the soiling capabilities of profiting from 'mere' trade, rather than 'actual labour.' In 1602 the Dutch East India Company was founded. This company received a Dutch monopoly on Asian trade and would keep this for two centuries. It would become the world's largest commercial enterprise of the 17th century. Spices were imported in bulk and brought huge profits, due to the efforts and risks involved and the insatiable demand (spices masked the taste of not so fresh food). In 1609 the Amsterdam exchange bank was founded, a century before its English counterpart." Today, by extending their business processes through the Internet, companies, remarkably similar to the Dutch East India Company, are making profits "out of thin air."

These new competitors are the *post-industrialists*. The first
wave of the Industrial Revolution saw the rise of the factory
as the way human work activity would be organized and
wealth produced. Factory workers became a new "middle-
class" supplanting the farm workers and encroaching on the
wealth held exclusively by the merchant class. With the need
for huge amounts of capital, industrialization brought with it
the rise of the "corporation" circa the 1800s, the emergence
of the first multinational companies, intellectual property
rights, limited liability companies, trade unions, commercial
banks, B-schools, and jobs outside the home for women.

Indeed, there is a new competitor on the block, ready to
engage your company in extreme competition. It's no longer
"business as usual," nor is this new competitor your father's
corporation.

As Peter Drucker once explained, "One thing is almost
certain: in the future there will be not one kind of corporation
but several different ones. The modern company was invented simultaneously but independently in three countries:
America, Germany and Japan. It was a complete novelty and
bore no resemblance to the economic organization that had
been the 'economic enterprise' for millennia: the small, privately owned and personally run firm. As late as 1832, England's McLane Report—the first statistical survey of business—found that nearly all firms were privately owned and
had fewer than ten employees. Forty years later a new kind of
organization with thousands of employees had appeared on
the scene, e.g., the American railroads, built with federal and
state support, and Germany's Deutsche Bank. Eighty years
ago, GM first developed both the organizational concepts
and the organizational structure on which today's large corporations everywhere are based. It also invented the idea of a

distinct top management. Now it is experimenting with a range of new organizational models. It has been changing itself from a *unitary corporation* held together by control through ownership into a group held together by management control, with GM often holding only a minority stake. GM now controls but does not own Fiat, itself one of the oldest and largest car makers. It also controls Saab in Sweden and two smaller Japanese car makers, Suzuki and Isuzu."

Since the modern corporation was invented, the basic business model has been that the corporation is the *master,* and the full-time employee, who could not make a living without the corporation, is its *servitor.* The corporation was designed to place all relevant activities under a single management to reduce "transaction costs" in producing goods and services. This was the model used by John D. Rockefeller in developing the Standard Oil Trust into the most profitable enterprise in business history, and a model perfected by Henry Ford.

The Ford Motor Company produced *everything:* the steel, engines, frames and tires. Ford was totally vertically integrated, owning rubber tree plantations in South America, and the railroad cars that delivered raw materials into its plants. And those same railroad cars shipped the finished products to market. Ford even had its own "factory police force" to monitor the men, and keep away people related to unions.

By most measures, the business model of the industrial corporation was yesterday, and now gone, as a result of key drivers of the great 21st century business reformation. Today, specialized knowledge workers are, in growing numbers, not even employees of the corporations they serve. They are *equals* in creating the means of production, not indentured minions of the corporation.

The vertically integrated corporation, owning the means of production from the rubber tree to automobile tire, has given way to *federations* of specialized companies (the Japanese call them *keiretsus*), where each participant has highly specialized skills, knowledge and resources. Today over 20 companies make up an average supply chain, reaching from raw material producer to the end consumer.

The "transaction costs" that once rationalized having all the value-delivery specialists under one roof (skyscraper) has been replaced with friction-free collaboration, made possible by the communications marvel, the Internet.

Super-specialized contract manufacturers can be located anywhere on the planet and contribute to the design, development and production of finished goods and services anywhere else on the planet (e.g., Dell or Levi Strauss with their contract manufacturers scattered across the globe). These new realities no longer apply to just the transnational corporations, but also to *individuals*, such as this author and his individual colleagues who researched this book from far away lands, including India, Japan, China, Korea, Singapore, Australia, Saudi Arabia, the Netherlands, and England.

Information is power. Also thanks to the marvel of our time, the Internet, the customer has the information, hence, the power, to demand what he or she wants, *when, where* and at *what cost.*

And the newly empowered customers demand that the goods and services they consume be bundled into ever more *complete solutions* to their needs, requiring that traditional companies step outside their once-tidy industries to meet the *complete* needs of their customers—a vacation is not an airline ticket, and airlines such as Virgin package the total vacation experience, not just the ride, for competitive advantage.

This means that industry boundaries are becoming blurred: a telephone is no longer just a telephone, it's a computer, a camera, a Web browser and a community of "friends and family circles."

Telecommunications no longer travels through copper wires and central office exchanges of the old-line phone companies. They now flow at broadband speeds across glass fibers and in the air through wireless technologies. Talk about industry blur, it was an invention from a glass company, Corning, that led to the fiber optic revolution of broadband communications. On the other hand, the invention of the transistor at Bell labs, a phone company, led to the rise of Sony and Panasonic in the consumer electronics industry. Industry boundaries are now increasingly blurred well beyond these two early examples.

Today, all companies must ask anew what business they are in, for if they don't, someone else will certainly get into their business. They had better be in the "customer business," aggregating total solutions to meet the ever growing demands of their customers. In today's world of oversupply and intense competition, *customers* are the only asset individual companies have left; therefore, they had better serve them well.

As a result of super-specialized knowledge flowing across industry boundaries, the classic R&D labs, like IBM's *self-contained* Thomas J. Watson Research Center or GE's first-ever industrial research labs that drove 19th-century invention and resulting business dominance for their owners, are now obsolete.

R&D is no longer taking place inside a single corporation, aimed at the knowledge base of a particular industry, but instead through alliances with entities outside any specific industry (e.g. Swatch, the high-fashion Swiss watch company designed Mercedes-Benz's new Smart Car, an acronym for *S*watch *M*ercedes *Art*).

The vertically integrated company serving a specific market, within a specific industry, with a specific product, is obsolete—dead, gone. Good bye, glass bottle industry, hello cardboard, plastic and aluminum. Good bye, copper cable industry, hello, glass fibers. Good bye to the vertically integrated company, hello to the company of the future.

The Five Transformers.

"Something is happening But you don't know what it is Do you, Mister Jones?"—Bob Dylan, Ballad of a Thin Man

Something is going on in business though it isn't clear exactly what. We are, perhaps, in the midst of one of the greatest business transformations ever in the industrialized world, a transformation that is being shaped by five key drivers: 1. knowledge as business capital, 2. the Internet, 3. jumbo transportation, 4. three billion new capitalists, and 5. the New IT, where business automation focuses on outward-facing business processes, not back office record keeping. Together, the results of these forces are far greater than the sum of the parts—and they are of historic proportions.

Knowledge as Business Capital. Princeton economist, Fritz Machlup, defined "knowledge work" and "knowledge industries" in his 1962 book, *The Production and Distribution of Knowledge in the United States,* in which he claimed the knowledge industry, representing 29% of the U.S. gross national product, as the beginning of the Information Age. He defined knowledge as a commodity and attempted to measure the magnitude of the production and distribution of this commodity within a modern economy. He also classified different kinds of knowledge, including intellectual knowledge and practical knowledge.

In 1973, sociologist Daniel Bell put forth the concept of a *post-industrial society* or *information age* in his book, *The Coming of Post-Industrial Society.* As creator of the concept of an *information society,* Bell reasoned that as we move from a manufacturer of goods to post-industrial society, theoretical knowledge, technology, and information become the major economic commodities. Those who know how to create, assemble, and disperse information are more valued than manual labor.

Useful information is expensive to create, but inexpensive to replicate—just consider a novel or a film. In *The Social Framework of the Information Society* (1980), through sheer insight, or perhaps fanciful thinking, Bell predicted that the emergence of a new social framework of telecommunications (which we now call the Internet) may be decisive for the way in which economic and social exchanges are conducted, the way knowledge is created and retrieved, and the character of the occupations and work in which men and women engage.

At about the same time as the Machlup writings, Peter Drucker claimed to have coined the term "knowledge worker" and asserted that knowledge workers, collectively, are the new capitalists.

He later went on to say, "Knowledge workers therefore see themselves as equal to those who retain their services, as 'professionals' rather than as 'employees.' The knowledge society is a society of seniors and juniors rather than of bosses and subordinates."[2]

As Drucker noted, "Within 20 or 25 years, perhaps as many as half the people who work for an organization will not be employed by it, certainly not on a full-time basis.

"Multinationals now tend to be organized globally along product or service lines. But, like the multinationals of 1913, they are held together and controlled by ownership. By contrast, the multinationals of 2025 are likely to be held together and controlled by strategy. There will still be ownership, of course. But alliances, joint ventures, minority stakes, know-how agreements and contracts will increasingly be the building blocks of a confederation. Increasingly, in the next society's corporation, top management will, in fact, be the company. Everything else can be outsourced." Oh my!

These new realities are certainly why China, India, and Ireland have made great sacrifices to invest in education, so that they can grow the knowledge workers of the future. China and India already turn out many times the number of science and engineering graduates as the U.S.

This Information Society is more than just technology. It includes social, cultural, institutional, moral, and political dislocations during our transition from a brute-force industrial society to a brain-force economy.

Specialized knowledge leads to a new kind of workforce with intellectual knowledge workers, such as scientists, able to claim an "intellectual capital" stake in wealth in the way that industrialists claimed a stake in wealth through monetary capital.

Just as skilled and semiskilled manual workers in factories represented a middle class in the 20th century, workers with specialized practical knowledge (engineers, technologists and technicians) are becoming the dominant economic force. Specialized schooling and certification will replace the apprenticeships of blue-collar workers of the past.

And, with the exception of tasks requiring that a technician work on site with their hands (X-ray technicians, nurses, physical therapists, psychiatric counselors, network cable installers and dental hygienists), such work can be carried out virtually anywhere (today lab tests for patients in New York are analyzed in New Delhi).

A hundred years ago, 95% of Americans worked with their hands and backs on the farm. Today, that number nears zero. Although manufacturing gave rise to America's economic might after World War II, today only around 15% of the workforce works in factories. So, where do we go from here?

Part of the answer to that question centers on what *kind* of knowledge will be needed in the years ahead. Because the blind continuation of the "hydrocarbon economy" will choke us all to death, learning to build an ecologically sustainable future is not only a good idea, it represents the knowledge base for "green innovation" that will underpin market leadership going forward. Tim Worstall's November 02, 2005 blog paints the picture, "The *China Daily* reported that China's 11th five-year plan, which starts soon, includes a program to sharply reduce China's energy usage per unit of G.D.P by 2010. In China, conservation is not a 'personal virtue,' as Dick Cheney would say. Today it is a necessity. It was so polluted in Beijing the other day you could not make out buildings six blocks away. Here's the good news: China's leaders know that as China grows more prosperous, and more Chinese buy homes and cars, it must urgently adopt green technologies; otherwise, it will destroy its environment and its people. Green technology will decide whether China continues on its current growth path or chokes itself to death. It may, indeed, already be too late, but green innovation is starting to mushroom in China.

"Green China will be much more challenging than Red China. Look around the nine-story Ministry of Science and Technology building. The porous pavement bricks are made of fly ash, a byproduct of coal combustion that allows storm water to flow through and be reabsorbed into the Beijing aquifer. Photovoltaic panels provide 10 percent of the building's electricity from sunlight? The hot water system is solar. The soil substitute in the building's roof garden is 75 percent lighter than regular dirt and holds three to four times more water per cubic foot. The concrete building blocks are filled with insulating foam that keeps you warmer in the winter and cooler in the summer. The urinals are water-free. All these green materials and products are, of course, 'Made in China.'

"A Chinese auto company is now rushing to develop a green diesel engine for passenger cars that will set the standards for the world. And what's the U.S. doing as green technology is emerging as the most important industry of the 21st century? Let's see: the Bush team is telling our manufacturers they don't have to improve auto mileage standards or appliance efficiency, is looking to ease regulations on oil refiners and is rejecting a gas tax that would help shift America to hybrid vehicles.

"Once they come up with low-cost solutions that work inside China, they will take them global at China prices. Get used to it. You think China is cleaning our clock now with cheap clothing? Wait a decade, when we'll have to import our green technology from Beijing, just as we have to import hybrid motors today from Japan." In the 21st century, the right kind of knowledge is the cornerstone of economic leadership.

The Internet. *Oh my, what can you say about the 20th century marvel, the World Wide Web? The Web presents an immense opportunity to connect every person, every computer, everywhere, across a company, across trading partners, across the globe. Such connectivity can revolutionize the very ways companies operate, the very ways they conduct business, leading to extreme efficiency and extreme effectiveness. But, even more revolutionary is that such connectivity can transform the very business a business is in.*—Keith Harison-Broniski, from the book, *Human Interactions.*

Now, all this knowledge industry stuff discussed in the section above may seem academic, but when you consider the wired world we live in today, some very interesting, and some really *big* things, start to happen.

Nobuyuki Idei, chairman and CEO of Sony, nets it out, "Broadband is comparable to the meteor that supposedly hit the earth 65 million years ago and wiped out the dinosaurs."[3] Is your company on the endangered species list? Is your country lagging behind in the availability of broadband?

As Assif Shameen reported in the magazine, *Chief Execu-*

tive, "It may be surprising to some that Korea is the world leader in broadband, because as recently as 1997 and 1998 it was undergoing what the Koreans call 'the IMF crisis.' That crisis, however, helped spark action. Now, South Korea is ground zero in the global broadband boom. In a country of 48 million people, there are 12 million broadband lines. Of the nearly 16 million Korean households, 78 percent now have a broadband connection—or more than four times the home broadband penetration rate of North America. (The United States has 21.5 million broadband connections serving 110 million households.) On average, Koreans spend more than 20 hours a week surfing the Internet. Korea has the world's highest rate of video- and movie-on-demand downloads. Not only is broadband ubiquitous in Korea, it is also much faster than elsewhere. At top speed, Korea's broadband connections over very high-bit digital subscriber lines (VDSL) are on average four times faster than the fastest broadband connections that the likes of Comcast, Time Warner or the Baby Bells provide in the U.S. over cable or the slower DSL modems. 'Within two and a half years, we expect more than 70 percent of our households will have Internet connections with access speeds of 20 megabits per second, which will allow them to download movies to watch on their high-definition TVs,' says Chin Daeje, Korea's minister of information and communications and a former Samsung Electronics executive. 'By 2010, the bulk of Korean households would have migrated to 100 megabits per second.'

"Now Chin is aiming to leverage Korea's leadership in broadband to open up a lead in other technologies, from home networking to digital media. He doesn't have any American ideological hang-ups about the relationship between government and business. He sees his role as chief facilitator for Samsung, LG, SK Telecom and KT to help them become dominant technology players. Although movies and videos on demand are still pie in the sky in the U.S. because of slow download speeds and high costs, they are a reality in Korea. For just 80 cents, you can download a Korean hit movie in not much more than a minute. 'What Apple's iTunes is doing to music in the U.S., broadband did to movies and TV archives in Korea two years ago,' says Lee Jae Woong, CEO of Daum, Korea's largest Internet portal."[4]

There's even more on the horizon for Korea's broadband leadership. Korea Telecom (KT) is creating a new WiBro (*Wi*reless *Bro*adband) network with the cell-to-cell roaming capabilities of regular cell phones. That means users can not only gain wireless broadband access from traditional WiFi or WiMax hot spots, Samsung, the world's third-largest cell phone vendor, has demonstrated that WiBro can also reach up to 2 Mbps inside a car moving at 120 kilometers per hour. Hmmm? Isn't America supposed to be the innovator and the most technologically advanced country? Caveat America.

Of even greater importance than movies and television shows is the impact that the broadband Internet will have on knowledge work. To understand the link between knowledge work and the Internet, a little background is useful. First, let's clear away some of the dot-com clutter associated with the Internet.

As the millennium clock rolled over to the 21st century, the Next Big Thing was thought to be the dot-com revolution, where everything business people knew was wrong, for the Internet had supposedly changed the very rules of business. Traditional business fundamentals were thrown out in favor of stratospheric initial public offerings (IPOs) of firms established by twenty-something year old entrepreneurs.

Arthur Clarke, author of *2001: A Space Odyssey,* helped explain the basis of much of the hype surrounding the dot-com e-commerce, e-business and e-everything, "Any sufficiently advanced technology is indistinguishable from magic."

Indeed the Internet had worked magic on public markets and there seemed no end in sight. That is, until the dot-com crash of 2000, the dot-bomb, where over an 18-month period the sucking sound could be heard, from San Jose to Wall Street, when almost three and a half trillion dollars evaporated as financial markets imploded.

Many thereafter concluded that the Internet fad was over. But, as this author wrote in *The Death of 'e' and the Birth of the Real New Economy,* the dot-bomb of 2000 wasn't the *beginning of the end,* it was the *end of the beginning.*

While those CEOs who didn't "get it" slammed the brakes on technology spending, others, like General Electric's storied CEO, Jack Welch, concluded that the impact of the Internet on business had just begun, for the Internet wasn't about a Web site or an IPO, it was all about a major business transformation—and that's where the link between knowledge as capital and the Internet intersect.

Actually, the fundamental concepts of manipulating information and managing sources of knowledge far precedes the Internet. In a 1945 article, "As we may Think" in *The Atlantic Monthly,* Vannevar Bush wrote, "The human mind operates by association. With one item in its grasp, it snaps instantly to the next that is suggested by the association of thoughts, in accordance with some intricate web of trails carried by the cells of the brain. It has other characteristics, of course; trails that are not frequently followed are prone to fade, items are not fully permanent, memory is transitory. Yet the speed of action, the intricacy of trails, the detail of mental pictures, is awe-inspiring beyond all else in nature."

Fast forward to the 1960s, where the communications medium was tightly linked to the content flowing across the medium. Famous for declaring that "the medium is the message," Marshall McLuhan foresaw changes that would bring about a new society characterized by greater connectivity and networking.

In his book, *Understanding Media,* (1964)[5] McLuhan writes, "The message of any medium or technology is the change of scale or pace or pattern that it introduces into human affairs. The railway did not introduce movement or transportation or wheel or road into human society, but it accelerated and enlarged the scale of previous human functions, creating totally new kinds of cities and new kinds of work and leisure. This happened whether the railway functioned in a tropical or northern environment, and is quite independent of the freight or content of the railway medium."

Paraphrasing McLuhan, the Internet accelerated and enlarged the scale of previous human information functions, creating totally new kinds of virtual and real cities, and new kinds of work and leisure, quite independent of the environment or the content of the medium.

Fast forward to the 1990s and putting teeth into Vannevar Bush's ideas, making his associations real with "hyperlink technology." To keep an eye on the standards of Web technology, Tim Berners-Lee created the World Wide Web Consortium (W3C) in 1994. While Apple Computer was the first to use hypertext with its *HyperCard* application in 1987, Berners-Lee took this to the next level by *networking* the hyperlinks on a grand scale. Thanks to Berners-Lee's World Wide Web —the hyperlinked Internet—knowledge work now knows no geographic boundaries. New information can move across the globe at the speed of light, in real time, and teams of knowledge workers can work together even though they are continents apart.

Boeing provides a world-class example of specialized knowledge work without bounds. Boeing designed its 777 in cyberspace, by electronically sharing design tools and processes with engineers, customers, maintenance people, project managers and suppliers across the globe. No physical model. No paper blueprints. The result is the slogan "The 777 is a bunch of parts flying together in close formation."

When you consider that knowledge is simply defined as "specific information about something," that is, it's specialized, that means the very brightest specialists in the entire world can be assembled to work together in real time on a single project.

GE has done exactly that by distributing its research labs across the globe with critical nodes in China, India and Germany. This author has done the same by assembling a team of researchers, including graduates of the world-famous Indian Institute of Technology, to research content for this book. This leads one to conclude that, in business, knowledge is after all, a new form of capital. For now, let's just say that we live in interesting times, where the Internet can network anyone, anywhere—moving the global economy into a period of thrashing, creative chaos. Don't be surprised if the next Bill Gates isn't eating some authentic curry in Chennai for lunch today, while Googling, via WiFi, of course. The bigger and more wired the world economy becomes, the more powerful individuals with specialized knowledge become.

Companies that may still think that the Internet is a fad, or at most the act of establishing a Web site to buy or sell goods or services, should read what one 90-year old senior citizen had to say in the *Atlantic Monthly* in 1999.

"The truly revolutionary impact of the Information Revolution is just beginning to be felt. But it is not 'information' that fuels this impact. It is not the effect of computers and data processing on decision-making, policymaking, or strategy. It is something that practically no one foresaw or, indeed, even talked about ten or fifteen years ago: the explosive emergence of the Internet as a major, perhaps eventually the major, worldwide distribution channel for goods, for services, and, surprisingly, for *managerial and professional jobs*. This is profoundly changing economies, markets, and industry structures; products and services and their flow; consumer segmentation, consumer values, and consumer behavior; jobs and labor markets. But the impact may be even greater on societies and politics and, above all, on the way we see the world and ourselves in it."

That was written by the father of modern management, the late Peter Drucker, who went on to compare the steam engine to the computer. "The steam engine was to the first Industrial Revolution what the computer has been to the Information Revolution—its trigger, but above all its symbol."

In 1776 the steam engine made it possible to mechanize the manufacturing process. By itself, the steam engine did not create the Industrial Revolution—it was necessary, but not sufficient. It was decades later that something totally unexpected happened. "In 1829, came the railroad, a product without precedent, and it forever changed the economy, society and politics." With the ability to distribute mass produced goods, the western world was engulfed by the biggest boom history had ever seen—the railroad boom. The railroad was the truly revolutionary element of the Industrial Revolution."[6]

The computer, itself, has not created the Information Age. Since its introduction in the 1940s, the computer has only transformed processes that were there all along. Now, decades after the advent of the computer, the Internet is to the Information Revolution what the railroad was to the Industrial Revolution. Hidden in plain sight from futurists of the 1990s, Internet technologies have let loose business change on a scale far greater than the computer itself. Historians will demark the Information Age, not by the advent of the computer, but instead by the advent of the Internet and its ability to create a single, virtual computer for all to share, all the time, from anywhere—one world, one information system, and one world wide workspace for knowledge workers.

And it won't just be cold data flowing through the Internet pipes. Dark fiber or unlit fiber is the name given to fiber optic cables which have yet to be used. The reason that dark fiber exists is that much of the cost of installing cables is in so called *civils*, the civil engineering work required in order to get the cables installed. This includes planning and routing, obtaining permissions, creating ducts and channels for the cables, and finally installation and connection. During the dot-com frenzy huge amounts of dark fiber was installed in anticipation of exponential demand around the globe. Subsequently, the collapse of the dot-com boom left fiber supply greatly exceeding even the most optimistically forecast, and the advent of wavelength division multiplexing further increased the capacity that could be placed on a single fiber by a factor of up to 100. As a result, the wholesale price of digital traffic collapsed, and a number of telecom companies filed for bankruptcy as a result. Their misfortune became the good fortune of others, and this overcapacity created a whole new telecommunications market. Now here's where this story gets interesting. Google is on a worldwide buying spree of dark fiber which analyst, Dave Burstein, thinks could ultimately support "the world's largest video server network," what he calls "the largest TV 'anti-network' in the world."

Burstein continues with an email to *San Jose Mercury News* writer, Michael Bazeley, "The key idea is that Google intends to become the most important video carrier on the planet, and is developing the servers and fiber network to make that possible. As television shifts to the Net, only Yahoo and perhaps British Telecom are in position to compete. The ABC's and NBC's of the world are outclassed. Google has told their folks to plan services as though the servers and delivery cost next to nothing." Speaking of broadband meteors hitting the Earth and wiping out dinosaurs, it won't just be television and movie industries disrupted by Google's free broadband. Every knowledge worker on the planet will be affected, and perhaps even commoditized, with $20,000-a-year PhDs at your fingertips. With broadband costing next to nothing, all is changed, changed totally.

But even greater bandwidth isn't the end of the story of what's to come with the Internet. The next giant leap is called the Executable Internet or X-Internet. The X-Internet overcomes the slow and cumbersome page-by-page download of information we've become so accustomed to with today's Internet. With the X-Internet, instead of pages of information, users are served programs that *execute* on the desktop computer (or cell phone or whatever), only going back to the server for little pieces as required by the activities of the user.

The X-Internet is precisely why Google strikes fear in the

heart of Microsoft, for Google isn't basing its future on its search engine, it's building the next-generation *computing platform,* wanting to supersede today's dominant Windows platform. Using a family of technologies called Ajax,[7] Google is making a huge investment in developing Web-based computer applications that have the richness and responsiveness previously only seen in desktop applications. For example, if you are using Google Maps, when you use your cursor to scroll around a map, everything happens almost instantly, with no waiting for pages to reload.

Even Microsoft's cash cow, its desktop application suite, Office, could be threatened with a new breed of productivity tools, such as OpenOffice.org, offered as a service by Google—for free. And that would only be the beginning as third party developers rush to build all manner of rich X-Internet applications. The X-Internet could also become the dominant computing platform for the bulky and cumbersome enterprise systems that run today's corporations. And with "the Internet is the software" approach, those dreaded and expensive upgrades are history—the latest version is always "just there" on the Net.

As George Colony, Chairman and CEO at Forrester Research, puts it, it's "Internet creative destruction, round two. Now you've got brains at both ends of the wire, resulting in a high-IQ, interactive, valuable conversation. Work is performed at both places, greatly increasing the richness of experience, the relevancy of content, and the amount that can get done."

It's not your father's Internet anymore. But, then again it may not wind up being Google's Internet anymore, either. While acknowledging the risks inherent in any start-up venture, Indian Internet pioneer, Rajesh Jain speaks eagerly of what he calls the phenomenon of the black swan—a rare, but not impossible, event. "Google was a black swan," he said. "No one expects the next Microsoft or Intel or Cisco to come out of India, but I believe it is entirely possible." Will Jain out-Google Google? Stay tuned.

The issues that businesses now face have never been larger or more imposing than those posed by the Internet and its potential to restructure the whole economy to achieve heretofore unattainable efficiencies and efficacies in getting work done. Traditional supply chains of the industrial economy are being transformed by "value chains of knowledge." The transformation is well under way—there is no turning back.

Jumbo Transportation. Today, this author, in steamy Tampa, Florida, ate some fresh honey-smoked wild Salmon from Alaska. Yesterday that very fish was in Alaska. It arrived overnight, packed in an iced-chilled box.

"Megalogistics," made possible by awe-inspiring jumbo jets and jumbo cargo ships, is a key driver of globalization, and just-in-time manufacturing. Just about anything can be shipped within 36 hours, from anywhere in the world, to anywhere in the world.

Except for products and services that are purely digital (e.g. software, information and music), the other side of the global commerce coin is physical distribution. Dennis Jones, former V.P. and CIO of FedEx explains, "What often gets lost in discussions about Internet commerce and the digital economy is the physical aspect of doing business. The Internet has engendered a feeling that anyone can start up a Web site to sell widgets, and instantly they're worldwide marketers. To succeed in Internet commerce, we believe a company has to be as effective in the physical world as it is in the electronic arena. The ability to move information around the world at the speed of light is a great enabler of commerce, but it breeds a corresponding need for the physical goods. The information network needs a physical network."[8]

While computers and the Internet capture our imagination as the greatest technological achievements of the 20th century, the taken-for-granted marvel of our times, and cornerstone of accelerating globalization, is the jumbo jet.

In 1980, U.S. commercial air carriers logged 7,255 Millions of Revenue-Ton-Miles. By 2000, that number had grown to 30,044, over half of which was international traffic.[9] Those statistics are for U.S. carriers alone, and with the rise of China as the world's workshop, logistics companies are in hot pursuit of providing greater cargo capacity.

Thirty years after launching the world's first twin-aisle, twin-engine jetliner, Airbus introduced its A380 as the first true double-deck passenger airliner for the long-range market. The A380 offers unprecedented levels of productivity, efficiency and economics in passenger service, while the A380-800F cargo version is to be the first commercial freighter with three full cargo decks. In passenger operations, the A380 retains significant cargo capability in its lower deck while accommodating 550-plus passengers on the two main decks (the maximum passenger load goes all the way to 840!). The A380's lower deck is designed to accept all standard underfloor cargo pallets and containers.

In its all-cargo version, the A380-800F will be the first commercial freighter with three full cargo decks—offering the unprecedented capability to carry a 150 ton payload over distances of 5,600 nm. This range enables the A380-800F to fly most major cargo routes non-stop, enhancing productivity by spending more time in the air. On a 5,000 nm. sector, the A380's direct operating cost is a full 21 percent lower than the largest competing freighter.

At a January, 2005 European media briefing, in Paris, Fred Smith, FedEx's CEO stated, "FedEx connects 95 percent of the world's Gross Domestic Product (GDP) in two to three business days. You might say we are the clipper ships of the 21st century. Now that the European Union has become China's biggest trading partner, you'll be interested to know that FedEx also provides the best network to China. Not only do we have more flights in and out of China than any other international air express company, but we also have several exclusive direct routes to the fast-growing Pearl Delta region, often called the source of the world's supply chain. We plan to serve another 100 new cities in China over the next few years and of course will use the new A380s to handle the expected traffic growth." [10]

And let's also not take for granted the jumbo cargo ship, that kicks in when jet speeds don't matter, but costs matters a lot. On July 11, 2005 Samsung Heavy Industries (SHI) handed over two completed 9,300 TEU (twenty-foot equivalent units) container ships to its client after holding a christening ceremony. SHI broke its own Guinness World Record in producing the world's largest ships since it had constructed 8,500 TEU container ships in July 2004. This proved the shipbuilder's possession of top technological ability in container ship innovation.

It took 16 months to complete the ships, with eight months spent in design and construction. Christened the MSC Pamelra and the MSC Susana, the two identical container vessels are 337 meters long and 46 meters wide, and will run between Europe and Asia. The ships can carry up to 9,200 units of 20 foot containers. This is equal to 1.2 million 29-inch color TVs or 50 million mobile phones each.

But there's more to the story of jumbo transportation than just moving stuff around the globe. Geoffrey James reported in the July 2004 issue of *Business 2.0* magazine: "When people think of UPS (UPS), they usually think of brown delivery trucks and guys in shorts dropping off packages. They do not think of laptop repairs. But that's exactly the business UPS has decided to enter. Toshiba is handing over its entire laptop repair operation to UPS Supply Chain Solutions, the shipper's $2.4 billion logistics outsourcing division. UPS will send broken Toshiba laptops to its facility in Louisville, Ky., where UPS engineers will diagnose and repair defects. Consumers will notice an immediate change. In the past, repairs could take weeks, depending on whether Toshiba needed components from Japan. But because the UPS repair site is adjacent to its air hub, customers should get their repaired machines back in just a matter of days."[11]

Meanwhile, FedEx now serves 190 cities in China, and plans to expand service to 100 additional cities within the next five years. Today, even the smallest company can have a global supply chain and world-class logistics support, allowing them to think globally and act globally.

While the Internet is clearly recognized as a marvel of modern business, extreme competition is also being driven by these physical marvels of *extreme logistics*. Globalization is a two-sided coin, with Internet connected knowledge work on one side, and extreme logistics on the other; both shrinking the world to where nations-state boundaries are being erased in a global economy. Opportunities—and challenges—of this shrinking world apply to huge corporations and sole proprietors alike.

Three Billion New Capitalists. The years 1979, 1989 and 1991 could be the most significant years in portending the world economy for the 21st century.

In July 1977, Deng Xiaoping was reinstated in all the Party and government posts he had been dismissed from during Mao Zedong's "cultural revolution." The Third Plenary Session of the 11th Central Committee held at the end of 1978 represented a great turning point of profound significance in the history of "New China." Since 1979, the focus has been shifted to modernization. Major efforts have been made to readjust the economic structure, and reform the economic and political systems.

China is, step by step, establishing a road leading to socialist modernization. Great changes have come about in China since 1979, and China is now the world's workshop, and soon to become a powerhouse of innovation.

In 1989, the Berlin Wall came tumbling down shifting the Soviet Empire into a market-driven group of independent nation states.

And in 1991, Manmohan Singh, the finance minister and now prime minister of India, moved the country to abandon Soviet-style central planning, massive bureaucratic socialist regulations, and steep tariffs blocking the import of state-of-the-art equipment, and opened up to free enterprise.

The result of these three watershed years is described at

length in Reagan administration trade official, Clyde Prestowitz's book, *Three Billion New Capitalists: The Great Shift of
Wealth and Power to the East* (2005). This is not a book of light
reading, or for the faint of heart, according its review in the
American Library Association's '*Booklist*' by Mary Whaley,
"Prestowitz, economic trend-spotter, reports, 'Over the past
two decades . . . China, India and the former Soviet Union all
decided to leave their respective socialist workers paradise
and drive their 3 billion citizens along the once despised capi-
talist road.' These new capitalists symbolize the threats to end
600 years of Western economic domination as America's lead
role in invention and technological innovation lessens and the
Internet allows jobs to be performed anywhere.

"The author foresees the possibility of an 'economic
9/11,' which won't kill but will cause great hardship. To prevent what he sees as an accident waiting to happen, Prestowitz offers a wide range of solutions relating to the dollar's
role in today's global marketplace, addressing the reality that
Americans consume too much and Asians save too much,
and facing energy challenges in the U.S and problems con-
fronting our educational system. The author offers valuable
insight into these important topics currently being debated in
government and corporate circles."

According to Prestowitz, "These new players are unusual. While having the low wages of developing countries, several hundred million of them have first world skills. That they are effectively next door and also planning to grow by exporting to U.S. markets dramatically increases the pressure on an already stressed system. Even for America there are ultimate limits on consumption and borrowing. U.S. borrowing already absorbs 80 percent of the world's available savings. President Bush says the U.S. economy is the envy of the world, and Federal Reserve Chairman Alan Greenspan insists economic growth is solid despite a bit of froth, but the truth is that the global economic scene is now more troubled that at any time since the trade wars with Japan 20 years ago. The U.S. trade deficit was considered unsustainable at around $25 billion annually by the Reagan administration. It is now nearing $700 billion, an unprecedented 6 percent of our gross domestic product. Former Federal Reserve Chairman Paul Volcker is forecasting a 75 percent probability of a major international financial crisis within five years."

As of 2005, the American government depends on Japan, China, the United Kingdom, Saudi Arabia, and Korea primarily to loan it money every day of the year. *New York Times* columnist, Paul Krugman, nets out what's happening with the American people, "these days Americans make a living by selling each other houses, paid for with money borrowed from China."[12] Is Greenspan suffering from "irrational exuberance" that's being driven by interest-only, variable-rate, no-money-down housing loans?

"Refinance and spend" has accounted for 90% of current American economic "growth" of the past few years, and 60% of homes bought in 2004 weren't to live in, but to "flip."

While Americans are cannibalizing their equity, and piling

up public and private debt, Asian countries are saving and investing in research, technology and education. In America, it's "party on, dude; shop until you drop," and it's summarized in the books titled, *Born to Buy*, and *The Overspent American*, by Harvard Professor, Juliet B. Schor.

In America it's about spending money. In China, India and Japan, it's about saving money. China and India are using their vast savings to offer investment incentives to lure high-tech companies such as Microsoft and Intel to their shores.

Prestowitz points out that in China and India the thinking goes beyond money and talent to *desire*: "Intel's CEO, Craig Barrett, is better known in China and India than Britney Spears. Barrett is feted by millions of Chinese at personal computer festivals. 'These people are crazy in love with technology,' says Barrett."

Prestowitz continues, "How, if the United States is the envy of the world, can we be having all these problems? According to our elite economists, America's future lies with high tech—with companies like Intel and IBM. Yet here are two of U.S. high-tech industry's top CEOs saying the future may lie abroad, especially in China. Add the fact that U.S. trade in high-tech products has swung from a surplus to a deficit, and it is not at all clear that this country's future will be in high tech. At the heart of the problem is the false assumption that all the countries in the globalization contest are playing the same game. They're not. Some countries have strategies, but others don't have a clue. The United States is in the latter category."[13]

There's much more to the story of China wanting Microsoft and Intel on their shores than just offering low-cost labor for these companies.

What happens when the world's richest man tries to dominate the world's most populated country? Well, even after a meeting with China's then president and "the man who changed China," Jiang Zemin, where Bill Gates agreed to reveal the Windows source code to Beijing to meet Chinese security demands, the Chinese go and develop their own distribution of the rival Linux operating system. It's called Red

Flag Linux, which opened the door for moving beyond just an indigenous operating system and on to the OpenOffice personal productivity suite that competes with the Microsoft Office suite. In a first step on the road ahead, a Beijing-backed consortium called China Standard Software Corp. is to buy up to one million Linux-based desktops from Sun Microsystems. Welcome to extreme competition, Mr. Gates. The Chinese don't want to just consume American designs, they want to be the innovators and climb their way into leadership in the high-end technology markets—and dominate.

When you think of the Gulf Cooperation Council (GCC) countries (Bahrain, Kuwait, Oman, Qatar, Saudi Arabia and the United Arab Emirates), you might tend to think of gushing oil wells and petrodollars, but little else, except, perhaps terrorism. Think again. The folks that gave us our numbering system and algebra are hard at work building a technological foundation for a 21st century economy. Omar Mark Ragel, Managing Director of BPM-Middle East tells another story, "During the last 30 years, I have witnessed many changes in the local market. In 1975, essentially the entire market was comprised of imported goods, and it was widely assumed that it would remain dependent on external sources for everything except crude oil and simple derivates such as gasoline and diesel. Dates were an export commodity since antiquity and have continued to be a popular trade item.

"The GCC region has experienced some good times, and quite a lot of trauma. The oil boom of the late 1970's and early 1980's saw per capita income surge to $14,000, only to experience the breathtaking slide to $4,000 by the early 1990's, when the price of oil dropped to a historic low of $9.00 per barrel. It is a great tribute to the social fiber that the resulting unemployment and underemployment didn't result in complete social upheaval. During that time the move to 'localize' products got under way by moving manufacturing facilities for fast-moving consumer goods into the region. The shift to local manufacturing was initially accomplished by licensing the market leaders for local production. For example, the clear market leader for dishwashing liquid was the U.K. brand, Fairy Liquid. With the product and its packaging being produced in the region, the retail cost dropped in half. There was no need to place protective tariffs on imports, for they were naturally excluded due to price competition."

In the early days, Saudi Arabia was totally dependent on imported fruit and vegetables. Not so today. The net inflow of capital to the region has supported the creation of a strong agricultural base that now exports flowers and salad bowl vegetables to Europe during the Winter, and sees Saudi Arabia as a net wheat exporter, encroaching on America as the breadbasket of the world.

The foreign fast-food invasion has been pretty well halted as indigenous organizations have stepped up to deliver consumers a highly attractive products wrapped in a health conscious message. McDonalds and Burger King are hard pressed today to compete with Kudu whole meal rolls and fresh grilled beef or chicken and fresh veggies, or with Dajen and Al-Tazaj fresh, locally produced chicken with world class delivery and highly competitive prices. Starbucks is facing strong competition from Dr. Café which is planning to expand into Europe and the U.S. with their scrupulous attention to detail to ensure consistent high quality product delivery at every outlet. In case you didn't know, "coffee" was discovered in the Kingdom of "Kaffa," an ancient state located in what is now Ethiopia. A popular legend refers to a goat herder by the name of Kaldi, who observed his goats acting unusually frisky after eating berries from a bush. Curious about this phenomena, Kaldi tried eating the berries himself. He found that these berries gave him a renewed energy. The news of this energy laden fruit quickly spread throughout the region. No one knows more about coffee than those in the Middle East—Starbucks be warned.

With its membership in the World Trade Organization, and strict protection of intellectual property rights, the market is acting as midwife to an embryonic software industry. Thirty years ago, the market withstood a 40% mark up on U.S. software price lists. Today the region is one of the low-cost software providers and a number of competence centers have been established, targeting delivery of skilled resources to Europe and the U.S. markets at 60% of established cost points. At the moment, Business Process Management (BPM) is rolling across the region as companies recognize the need to interact with other businesses across a wide spectrum of industries, across the globe, from petrochemicals, to agriculture, to tourism, to business process outsourcing.

Ragel explains the current investment situation in the Gulf states, "Recent political threats, and the imposition of a massive regime of investment restrictions by the current U.S. administration, has seen billions of dollars pulled out of Western financial markets and brought home, where it has found a bright, creative and energetic 21st century business environment. Projects range from the world's largest shrimp farms, producing high quality, low cost shrimp for world markets, to Dubailand, which will contain 45 mega projects and over 200 tourism, leisure and entertainment sub projects, making it the most ambitious tourist destination ever created. Dubailand is being created to appeal to the widest audience of tourists, covering all age groups, nationalities and activities. On completion, Dubailand will be the largest theme park *ever*, twice the size of the Walt Disney World Resort in Orlando, Florida.

All in all, this region may be one of the best kept economic secrets today. Don't be surprised if you wake to find Dajen replacing your local Kentucky Fried Chicken, or Dr. Café supporting your craving for a tasty cappuccino. The three billion new capitalists are not all from China and India.

Dubailand

But the region isn't just going beyond oil to coffee and entertainment. It too has its eyes set on knowledge work. Dubai Internet City provides a Knowledge Economy Ecosystem that is designed to support the business development of Information and Communications Technology (ICT) companies. It is the Middle East's biggest IT infrastructure, built inside a free trade zone, and has the largest commercial Internet Protocol Telephony system in the world.

Dubai Internet City is a strategic base for companies targeting emerging markets in a vast region extending from the Middle East to the Indian subcontinent and Africa, covering 2 billion people with a GDP of $ 6.7 trillion. It's in Dubai these days where you'll find Arab investors who have pulled billions of dollars out of Western financial markets meeting with Indians and Chinese to reallocate those investments.

In line with Dubai's liberal economic policies and regulations, Dubai Internet City offers foreign companies 100% tax-free ownership, 100% repatriation of capital and profits, no currency restrictions, easy registration and licensing, stringent cyber regulations, and protection of intellectual property.

Intel's Craig Barrett at Dubai Internet City in 2002

The global ICT giants are all there: Microsoft, Oracle, HP, IBM, Compaq, Dell, Siemens, Canon, Logica, Sony, Ericsson and Cisco, to name just a few. These companies represent a formidable community of over 5,500 knowledge workers.

The cluster of ICT companies in Dubai Internet City are comprised of software development, business services, e-commerce, consultancy, education and training, sales and marketing, and back office operations. DIC provides a scalable state-of-the-art technology platform that allows companies looking to provide cost effective business process outsourcing (BPO) services such as call center operations.

The "global village" is a term, coined by Marshall McLuhan in his 1962 book *The Gutenberg Galaxy*, describing how electronic mass media collapse space and time barriers in human communication, enabling people to interact and live on a global scale. In this sense, the globe has been turned into a village by the electronic mass media.

Today, the global village is mostly used as a metaphor to describe the Internet and World Wide Web. The Internet globalizes communication by allowing people and computers from around the world to connect with each other. This new reality has implications for forming new economic and social structures being shaped by three billion new capitalists. Globalization doesn't just mean offshoring jobs to India and China; it means we've crossed the threshold to a whole new economic world order, all across the third rock from the Sun. Business will never be the same—so, get used to it.

The New IT. In 2003, the infamous article, "IT Doesn't Matter," splashed onto the pages of the *Harvard Business Review*, and subsequently got used in boardrooms across America as ammo for deep IT budget cuts.

Even though General Electric's CEO, Jeff Immelt, called

the article "stupid" the great IT backlash had begun—IT spending flip flopped from the late 1990s stupendous overspend that was driven by the dot-com frenzy, to the current under spend, driven by IT-wary business executives. The article set forth the following New Rules for IT management: "Spend less; follow, don't lead; and focus on vulnerabilities, not opportunities."

But, now it's time for another IT flip flop, and here's why: the outsourcing of white-collar work and the growing trend of multi-company alliances.

While many Boards of Directors' members were lulled to sleep by that HBR article, and were dreaming of huge IT cost savings, India, China, Russia, and Eastern Europe were burning the midnight oil opening up a whole new trend toward outsourcing and offshoring that no business wanting to remain competitive can ignore. With the far away brought to our desktops by the Internet, Shanghai and San Francisco, Chennai and Chicago, and Boston and Bangalore are now next-door neighbors.

It won't be just the satellite/fiber networks that drive the continued globalization of highly skilled white-collar workers, it will be the ability to create *virtual work spaces* where far flung teams can work together in real time. As globalization continues, the demand for a new generation of technology support for work accomplished by geographically dispersed teams becomes clear.

Contrary to the HBR article, it's not time to constrict the role of IT, but to expand it—and innovate in ways not possible prior to the advent of universal Internet connectivity. However, it's not the kind of IT known as data processing or transaction processing or record keeping, as cited in the HBR article. It's not the kind of IT that, as the article correctly points out, companies blindly threw money at during the dot-com frenzy, thinking it would magically deliver competitive advantage. It's IT of a different kind. You can think of this badly needed new category of *business-interaction technology,* Business Process Management (BPM), as *the New IT,* technology that animates human work and business process collaboration, similar to the way that software animates computer hardware.

The Old IT applied automation to information; the New IT applies automation to *relationships.* The Old IT was about keeping records and transmitting data; the New IT is about *"connecting and collaborating"* to get work done—now that productivity doesn't require proximity.

The New IT requires a new kind of leadership, the Chief Process Officer (CPO), not the traditional Chief Information Officer (CIO), whose chief concerns were mostly the management of technical assets. To this extent, the HBR article is certainly correct, traditional IT, *the Old IT,* doesn't matter, for this form of IT is indeed a commodity. The new CPO's chief concerns will be in providing a technology-enabled capability to manage a company's business process assets and support the ability for knowledge workers to "connect and collaborate" inside and outside the walls of their companies.

"Uh oh," you may be thinking, "please don't let this book drop into techno-speak." So, let's set the stage with a simple discussion of how BPM will become as everyday and assessable to all, as email is today. Even grandma doesn't fear or shy away from email, for it helps her "stay in touch" with her grandchildren scattered around the country, and some around the globe. So, please bear with this author for just a minute as we demystify BPM and explain how it can help companies "stay in touch" with their customers and suppliers.

Think of BPM as simply *technology-enabled support for business interactions,* much like email is technology-enabled support for business communications. If we look at BPM more closely, it becomes obvious that its power is its capability to revamp the interactions among a company's suppliers, trading partners and customers almighty.

With BPM, events, or requests by customers, can trigger processes across trading partners located in, let's say, New York, New Delhi, and Taipei. *These business processes interact so seamlessly that it appears that they are all being handled by a single system, a single company, rather than by an alliance of companies acting as one.* BPM supports both system-to-system (S-2-S) interactions and, increasingly, human-to-human (H-2-H) interactions.

There are those who would argue now that the world-wide interconnectivity of people and computer systems through the Internet will transform what it means to be a business and what it takes to win at business. But it's not just the possible connections between people and computers that's important, it's how companies redefine and reorganize their *work* and organizational structures to take advantage of that connectivity that counts. That's precisely where BPM business software comes in. For large and small companies alike, BPM can fundamentally change the ways they operate—and operational innovation is the secret sauce of competitive advantage in the ever-rising global economy.

The results of having BPM capabilities are profound and will directly effect the firm's profitability and survivability. Companies will be able to provide customers what they want, when they want it, and where they want it, at a price they are willing to pay.

By orchestrating the activities of suppliers who work in parallel, cycle times can be reduced from weeks or months to hours or minutes. Each participant in a supply chain can optimize its work as customer-generated events and market activities are known to all in real time.

Productivity soars as manual work is reduced and human errors eliminated, leaving humans to concentrate on the exceptions that only humans can handle. Customer satisfaction climbs as errors and inefficiencies are wrung out of customer service, and process-powered self-service allows customers to become more self-reliant in solving problems.

But BPM isn't something a company can just go out and buy. Buying a word processor won't make its owner a novelist. Email won't make its user have something interesting to say. BPM must not be considered as just another "product" IT vendors will be happy to sell. Properly understood, BPM is a technology-enabled way of running a business. On the other hand, it's not business as usual, for the process-managed company with technology-enabled BPM capabilities will have the agility to stay one step ahead of the competition and set the pace of innovation in global markets.

With the New IT, BPM, harnessing the universal connectivity of the Internet, a whole new world of business possibilities open up. Consider, for example, when airline industry veteran, David Neeleman, decided to bring humanity back to air travel. He had to transform how an airline could operate so that it could do the seemingly impossible: offer extremely low fares, while delivering a high quality product that would delight travelers. Taking on this challenge, he created JetBlue.

One example of how he slashed costs was through transforming the reservation process. He cut out commissions to travel agents, and, instead of paying high rent and corralling reservationists into cubicles, he let them stay home, and let the Network become their JetBlue offices. This operational innovation meant no expensive real estate; no expensive time-wasting, harrying commutes; and lots of happy reservationists—just call and ask them.

Now let's turn to Clyde Prestowitz's account of where his new PC came from, "I just bought a new IBM laptop computer. I traced the root of my computer. It is an interesting journey. The computer has a Pentium chip, which began as a cylinder of silicon in Korea that FedEx carried to Albuquerque, New Mexico, where it was turned into a wafer. That wafer then went back to Albuquerque Airport, to San Francisco, to Narita, to Penang, Malaysia, where it was cut, assembled, and tested. It then went to Zhuhai, China, where it met up with the flat panel that was coming in from Japan and the hard drive that came in from Singapore and the memory chips that came in from Taiwan. It was all assembled by a company called Flextronics, which, probably, none of you have ever heard tell of, which is the actual assembler and manufacturer not only of my IBM ThinkPad, but of your HP printers and lots of other things that have other people's labels on them—Dell computers and so forth.

"Then it flew from Zhuhai to Shanghai, got on FedEx Flight 24 from Shanghai to Memphis, seventeen-and-a-half hours, sorted out, on another plane, and at my house at 11:30 in the morning. It took four days for me to get my computer. All those materials went through that loop in those four days. That is how the system of globalization works today."

All Prestowitz, the customer, had to do was simply order an IBM Thinkpad by clicking on his computer mouse to trigger this dance of interacting business processes across umpteen companies and umpteen countries. Technology-enabled business process management, this "New IT," is a cornerstone of competitive capabilities needed in the 21st century.

What Does All This Mean?

In response to the five forces driving the great 21st century business reformation, companies must come to grips with 16 realities of extreme competition.

1. Extreme Customers

"Whoever has the information has the power. Power is thus shifting to the customer, be it another business or the ultimate consumer. Specifically, that means the supplier, e.g., the manufacturer, will cease to be a seller and instead become a buyer for the customer. This is already happening." – Peter Drucker.[14]

Information is power. The power shift from *producer* to *consumer* is well underway, thanks in large part to the informating[15] power of the Internet. Since the millennium clock rolled over to the 21st century, businesses are being buffeted by a silent revolution and a power shift in global markets. Armed with networked information technology, the customer has grabbed power from producers. It is now the fully informed, never satisfied customer that holds absolute power in the marketplace, determining what is to be made, when, where and at what cost.

And, today's customers want it all, not just the buying transaction. Whether it is buying a PC, spare-parts, engineering services or life insurance, customers want complete care throughout the consumption life cycle—from discovery all the way through support after the sale or contract.

Today, customers demand the best deal, the best service, and solution-centered support. The Industrial Age was about mass production. The Customer Age is about mass customization. It is about turning a company, and its entire value chain, over to the command and control of customers—and earning their loyalty! In both business-to-consumer and business-to-business markets, owning the customer, the whole customer, is the "prize" of 21st century business.

Of course, no one "owns" customers, who are but a mouse click away from the competition. But the goal remains the same—instead of owning the product and pushing it to market segments, winning 21st century companies will seek to position themselves directly in the path of greatly empowered customers as they pull products and services from a multitude of suppliers to meet their individual needs. As Drucker put it, suppliers won't sell to customers, they will become buyers for them.

As control of markets and economies shifts from the producer to the consumer, the secret is to customize offerings, one customer at a time. The company that wants to win understands that, when it comes to customers, the key is no longer making the sale, "the transaction," it's the relationship that counts. Caveat Venditor (seller beware)! The ultimate challenge is about earning customer *loyalty*.

Cambridge Technology Partners' Joe Giffler explains,[16] "We've all heard the statistics about customer loyalty:

- "...the average company loses half its customers over a five year period..."
- "...reducing defections 5% can boost profits from 25% to 85%..."
- "...yet companies typically spend five times more on customer acquisition than on retention..."
- "...65% to 85% of customers who defect say they were satisfied with their former supplier..."
- "...totally satisfied customers are six times more likely to repurchase than satisfied customers"
- "...a happy customer will tell five people about their ex-

perience, while each dissatisfied customer will tell nine..."

Michael Meltzer, NCR Corporation's former director for financial services consulting, has made some interesting observations about Pareto's Law. "Pareto's Law, also called the 80/20 rule, makes the observation that 80% of the profit is derived from 20% of the customers. While Pareto's Law is considered by some to be naive and overly simplistic, this 80/20 relationship appears too often to be ignored. In the past, it was always easier to attempt to 'poach' your competitors' customers. However, studies have shown that companies spend five times more money on acquiring new customers as they do on retaining those they already have. Further studies demonstrated that: 'As a customer relationship with a company lengthens, profits rise[17]—and not just a little. Companies can boost profits by 100% by retaining just 5% more of their customers.'"[18]

The winning strategy is to segment customers with the 80/20 rule, and then invest in real-time 1-to-1 marketing and lifetime customer care with the 20%, most productive market segment. the goal is to create communities-of-interest, and provide solution-centered knowledge resources.

Companies must listen and learn what these customers want and find ways to meet those needs, now and in the future. The 20% club is not static. In both B-to-B and B-to-C market spaces, customer needs change over time. By blending sales force automation (SFA) with customer self-service, a new generation of marketing strategy can be implemented for competitive advantage. And since the customer and the sales force can have a 360° view of each other, true customer partnerships can be forged.

Marketing guru, Regis McKenna describes customer partnerships, "Ultimately, marketing should involve the customer as a partner in development and production. It won't be easy to do, because most companies today have focused their processes on improving time to market and, by inclination and culture, see the customer as an end target rather than a partner."

Investing in the top 20% of customers does not mean closing doors. Cambridge Technology Partners' Paul McNabb and Mike Steinbaum explain, "Of course, the door for new customers is always open, but the less glamorous areas of customer care often pay higher returns. The effort required to further develop existing relationships is often quite small compared to the potential payoff. Existing customers represent the 'low-hanging fruit' because a relationship has already begun. And loyal customers are an enterprise's best customers. Each year a customer remains with the company, his or her value increases—spending tends to go up. Also, existing customers are often the best source of referrals."

Kevin Kelly, Senior Maverick at *Wired* magazine and author of *Out of Control and the New Rules for the New Economy* explains, "The central economic imperative of the Industrial Age was to increase productivity. The central economic imperative of the network economy is to amplify relationships. Since a relationship involves two members investing in it, its value increases twice as fast as one's investment. Outsiders act as employees, employees as outsiders. New relationships blur the role of employees and customers to the point of unity. They reveal the customer and the company as one. In the network economy, producing and consuming fuse into a single verb: *prosuming*. And whoever has the smartest customers wins.

"The world's best experts on your product or service don't

work for your company. They are your customers, or a hobby tribe. The network economy is founded on technology, but can only be built on relationships. It starts with chips and ends with trust."

Kelly has done a magnificent job of netting out the strategic goals of getting closer to your customers:

- "Make customers as smart as you are.
- Connect customers to customers.
- All things being equal, choose technology that connects.
- Imagine your customers as your employees.
- Don't just solve problems; pursue opportunities."[19]

Because the goal in the Customer Age is about gaining customers for life, it is about a conversation, an interactive dialog and shared know-how, not a transaction.

In his keynote at Neosphere 98, Bob McCashin, EDS Corporate VP, summed up the power shift to the customer, and the need for enterprise customer management, "We are entering a new era—or perhaps it is the rebirth of an older one—in which the individual customer is central. It is an era of understanding, or intimacy, with the people we serve— even when they live on the other side of the world. It's a time when we can know hundreds of thousands of customers well—particularly our best customers. And we can show them that we appreciate their business in meaningful ways. It's called 'enterprise' because market leaders today realize that all forms of interactions with their customers—whether through sales, service, or delivery—affect their customer relationships. These interactions can help you acquire the right customers—retain them by meeting their individual needs— and maximize the lifetime value of the most profitable customer relationships."[20]

In the Customer Age, customers become first-class business assets, to be managed with the same care as traditional assets such as capital and labor. Like other business assets a company must *invest* in its productive customers to achieve maximum value. Classifying customers by their lifetime value (LTV) to the enterprise can guide the investment in building relationships.

Cambridge Technology Partners explains, "Customer relationships are assets that require investment in order to reach full potential. The enterprise must determine which relationships are worth the investment and how to get the highest return from each one. Since building relationships is not a cost-free proposition, customers with the highest potential to perform should receive the most attention. For one-time customers as well as 'churners,' who display little loyalty despite all attempts to retain them, close relationships may represent losing investments. Personalized customer care makes sense if the customer's lifetime value sufficiently exceeds the cost of building the relationship."[21]

How does a company really get close and stay close to customers in the world of automation? For one thing, it must overcome the problem of capturing and processing new kinds of information. An enterprise needs to make a quantum leap in its information systems—from handling *transactions* to handling *conversations* —collecting and processing behavioral data.

Rich Melmon, Partner in The McKenna Group, explains the essential elements of the right kind of customer dialog, "If these [customer] dialogues are designed properly, they will allow a wide range of people with varying needs to find their way through the system easily to get what they come for. From the user's point of view, the dialogues will integrate four basic elements:

- *Personalization:* I want it my way, with my particular needs

driving the system's responses to me
- *Self-service:* I want to explore on my own, select on my own, and troubleshoot on my own
- *Immediacy:* I want the information now; I want the product now
- *Intimacy:* I want it to feel like a two-way process; I want to know that my actions are being used by the company to learn what I want; I want my feedback to register with the company; and I want tangible evidence that I'm in the loop.[22]

The idea of deeply knowing your customer is not new, but the idea of actually doing something about it and making it the center of your thinking appears to many to be new and radical. One of the best examples of how such knowledge can change fortunes and, indeed, industries, comes from the airlines industry. Much is written about the strategies and successes of companies like South West Airlines and JetBlue in the U.S., EasyJet and Ryan Air in the U.K. and Virgin Blue in Australia. What is not really talked about it is the fact that much of the great work around customer centric strategy was actually derived from Scandinavian Airlines (SAS) and is encapsulated in the book, *Moments of Truth: New Strategies for Today's Customer-Driven Economy,* by former CEO Jan Carlzon.

In the 1980s, Carlzon almost single handedly turned SAS around and made it a major carrier. In Carlzon's words, "At SAS we used to think of ourselves as the sum total of our aircraft, our maintenance bases, our offices, and our administrative procedures. Then thinking about it through the eyes of the customer SAS realized that, in fact, it was not a collection of material assets at all, instead SAS was defined by the quality of their contact between individual customers and the SAS employees who serve the customer directly. Each of SAS's 10 million customers come into contact with approximately five SAS employees, and this contact lasts an average of 15 seconds each time. Thus, SAS is "created" 50 million times a year, 15 seconds at a time." Carlzon concludes that these contacts are 50 million "Moments of Truth" that ultimately decide whether SAS will succeed or fail as a company. Building out from those "Moments of Truth" (MOT) we can see that each of them provides two opportunities. Either it can become a "Moment of Magic" where we excel and delight the customer, or a "Moment of Misery" where we disappoint the customer at best, and, at worst, completely alienate them. So, without deep knowledge of our customer, do we have any way of knowing whether we are delivering Moments of Magic or Moments of Misery? The advice is to understand all those MOT's and then ensure that they create Magic.

Delighting the customer doesn't necessarily mean pampering, or that the customer is always right. In a recent U.K. "Fly on the Wall" documentary, low-cost Ryan Air's Chief executive Michael O'Leary was actually heard swearing at a passenger and telling him to go away and never use the airline again! The passenger's crime? Well he was extremely abusive to the check-in staff over a delayed flight and was complaining that he was going to miss an extremely important business meeting as a result. O'Leary was basically telling the passenger that if it was so critical that he was there at that time, and if he expected premier service, then perhaps he should consider paying the full fare of a premier service airline! This may sound very harsh, but for Ryan Air, its aim is to offer low-cost air travel for people who want it, and that also means people who are willing to understand the associated risks. Ryan Air is not trying to deliver a premier business service on the cheap.

What's important for any company is to determine the life-time value (LTV) of its *productive* customers; and slavishly serve those customer with precisely what they want, and not fret over losing customers that cost money, rather than make money, for the company. A company cannot be all things to all customers, so the LTV of customers must be the central part of the equation of a company's business model.

CEO of the non-profit Business Process Management Group, Steve Towers, summarizes, "You will have heard the phrase 'the customer is always right.' Well that's not true, at least not in the way that is often used: '*every* customer is always right!' Some companies are so knotted up with pleasing everybody that they are unable to fully service the needs of the customers that are most important to them. There are always customers who don't fit well with what a company is trying to do, so be prepared to lose them, so that you can better focus on the customers that you do want. If that sounds like heresy then think in terms of custom rather than customer—there are certain needs that you can't or don't want to meet. It's not the individual that you are dismissing."

If you focus on your most productive customers, and "Hug Your Customers," as suggested in the book by that title, penned by Jack Mitchell, CEO of two high-end clothing stores in Connecticut, some amazing things start to happen. Customers will want to buy more and more from your company. For example, the Virgin Group of companies originally started out in the music business as a record company. The group now spans many industries. The Virgin Group has created over 200 companies worldwide, employing over 35,000 people. Its total revenues around the world in 2004 exceeded $8.1 billion.

Interestingly Virgin's decision to go into a business sector is made on two primary factors: 1. Is the customer in that sector getting a raw deal? and 2. Would the goods or services appeal to the customers we already serve?

These Virgin people are crazy about *exceeding* their customers' expectations. What's better than watching a really great movie? Watching a really great movie with an ice cream! That's what Virgin thought too, which is why Virgin Atlantic dishes out choices to passengers while they're watching movies onboard. And forget the hug, get a complete body massage while crossing the Atlantic in Upper Class. Once at Virgin Money, one of its customers really didn't want to be put on hold, so a call center operator sang "New York, New York" to him while he waited to find out some information.

What business is Virgin really in? The "customer business." Virgin listens carefully to its present and future customers, and gives them what they want, how they want it, even if that means starting a new business to do so.

TAKEAWAY: The power shift from *producer* to *consumer* is well underway, thanks in large part to the "informating" power of the Internet. Armed with networked information technology, the customer has grabbed power from producers. It is now the fully informed, never satisfied customer that holds absolute power in the marketplace, determining what is to be made, when, where and at what cost. As noted by management authority, Peter Drucker, the producer of products and services will cease to be a seller and, instead, become a buyer for the customer. To compete in the 21st century, a company must shift from being a product-driven company to a becoming a customer-driven company that is laser-focused on its customers to the point where the company can anticipate customers' needs, even before they do.

2. Extreme Innovation

Innovative ideas are easy; doing them is hard. Surrounded on the one side by extreme, never-satisfied customers, and three billion new capitalists playing hardball on the other, Bruce Nussbaum has some advice in *Business Week*'s August 1, 2005 issue, "Listen closely. There's a new conversation under way across America that may well change your future. If you work for Procter & Gamble or General Electric, you already know what's going on."

For over five years, this author has written about the globalization of white-collar work as the new trend beyond the established trend of sending blue-collar jobs to Asia and beyond. Even much of the so-called "service economy" and the "knowledge economy," once thought of as the last bastions of America's economic might, have been digitized and beamed to China, India, Russia and beyond. In short, knowledge work is being digitized, globalized and commoditized. So, what's left for companies wanting to avoid commodity purgatory? Welcome to the *Innovation Economy.*

Nussbaum describes the notion of an innovation economy, "The new forms of innovation driving it forward are based on an intimate understanding of consumer culture—the ability to determine what people want even before they can articulate it. Working in what is still the largest consumer market in the world gives U.S. companies a huge edge. So does being able to think outside the box—something Americans still do better than most. But Toyota Motor Corp. has a feel for U.S. consumers, and the Samsung Group can be pretty creative, too. Competition will surely be intense."

"You're thinking 'this is all hype,' aren't you? Just another 'newest and biggest' fad, right? Wrong. Ask the 940 senior executives from around the world who said in a recent Boston Consulting Group Inc. survey that increasing top-line revenues through innovation has become essential to success in their industry." Nussbaum also reports that nearly 96% of all innovation attempts fail to beat targets for return on investment, leading to talk of "innovation frustration" in the corner offices.

So where does innovation come from? One answer lies in the notion of *clusters.* American innovation isn't restricted to the research labs of the big companies or the famous universities located there. America innovates to the extent it does because there is a cluster of technologists who live in concentrated areas, e.g. Silicon Valley or Boston's Route 128, and frequent the same bars. As international software development and R&D clusters are moved to China, India, Russia and Korea, innovation will follow and increasingly become stateless.

In 2004, China began speaking of technological nationalism, meaning that the country wants to create autochthonous technologies and standards, making innovation an indigenous national asset, not an import. The Chinese don't just want to make what Americans innovate, they want to innovate and dominate global markets with their innovations.

But wait, what exactly is innovation? A dictionary definition doesn't help much: 1: the introduction of something new, 2: a new idea, method, or device. Most often the tendency, when pondering what innovation is, is to think of a glitzy new product with bling, such as Apple's iPod. But when we think of innovation as the Next Big Thing in business, we need to understand it in a business context that includes many variables besides product innovation.

Business innovation has multiple dimensions that interact to form a true breakthrough for competitive advantage. Further, the word "innovation" is problematic. Strictly speaking, an innovation is something *completely new,* but there is, practically speaking, no such thing as an unprecedented innovation in business or technology. Even in the world of science, true scientists will tell you of an invention accredited to them as really acts of "climbing on the shoulders of others"—their peers and predecessors.

With business innovation, it's usually about "connecting the dots" across the major types of business innovation to create something distinctive, something new, especially as perceived in the eyes of a company's customers. It's also about connecting the dots between unique business practices in other industries.

British business process consultant, Mark McGregor, describes how best practices can be drawn from several industries to create what he calls *next practices,* "What if you looked to brand-based companies such as Coca Cola for your ideas on marketing, what if you looked at someone like Amazon for your inspiration in building on-line shops for your products, and possibly someone like McKinsey as your inspiration for providing service? I am sure you will agree that a company that delivered products to the same quality as a pharmaceutical company and services to the standard of McKinsey, while being as smart at brand awareness as Coca Cola and as easy to buy from as Amazon—would cause more than a few ripples in its marketplace."[23]

Returning to the idea that there are several major types of business innovation, let's set some context. At a high level, the simplest of business models is buy-make-sell. Thus companies have three key activities. They buy goods and services from suppliers. They add value to these inputs to make something of greater value than the sum of the parts, the inputs. Then they sell the good or service, hopefully at a margin that reflects the value added. That value is the value perceived by the customer, not just the sum of the costs of the parts that go into the good or service.

All of the buy-make-sell activities of a company consist of two types: *direct activities* that see the goods progress from acquiring the inputs through to producing and delivering the final product or service; and *indirect activities* that are essentially support activities, including facilities management, human resource administration, financial management, repairs, maintenance and so on. Direct activities ultimately touch the customer; indirect activities don't; hence the term, indirect.

All of these activities are objects of potential innovation, taking us way beyond the simplistic notion that business innovation only equates to product innovation—which is usually an invention of some sort.

Everyone associates Thomas Edison with the light bulb. So strong is that association that many people actually assume that Edison actually invented the light bulb, whereas it was, in fact, invented by a man named Joseph Swann in Sunderland in the U.K. What Edison and his team did was to perfect the light bulb and to create demand for such a product. It was Edison's "business innovations" that made money, not Swann's invention. Xerox's Palo Alto Research Center (PARC) invented many of the technologies behind today's Macintosh PCs; it was Apple Computer that made the money. In other words, product invention is but one type of "business innovation."

A more complete list of business innovation categories include:

- Operational innovation
- Organizational innovation
- Supply-side innovation
- Core-competency innovation
- Sell-side innovation
- Product and Service innovation.

Operational Innovation. Why is it that, given two companies with approximately the same assets and number of skilled employees, one struggles and the other grows profits? From where do those profits come? The answer is that they come from how work gets done: how companies *do* what they do, how they operate. Operational innovation is the next frontier of business advantage. Lacking growth markets, and facing global competition in uncertain times, companies must change the way they conduct business—or competitors that reinvent *their* operations will run circles around them. It's about operational transformation, time-based competition, and flawless execution of business strategies. Wal-Mart operates with awe-inspiring efficiency because it innovated real-time inventory control, cross-docking of supplier inbound trucks and Wal-Mart outbound trucks at it distribution centers. Progressive, the auto insurer, launched a fleet of vans and provided its claims adjusters with laptop computers so that they could settle most claim in nine hours compared to the 7-10 days that was best practice in the industry.

Operational innovation isn't about improving *what* your company currently does, it's about transforming *how* you do what you do in order to distinguish yourself in your industry.

Organizational Innovation. The days of the vertically integrated company are over. The efficiencies of having a company carry out all of its activities by itself simply aren't there any more. Instead, companies will, more and more, become laser-focused on their core competencies, and build alliances with the best-of-the-best specialists to do the rest.

Organizational innovation can be used to redistribute internal resources, from non-core to core activities. Organizational innovation can increase a company's flexibility in responding to changes in the marketplace, and can help to eliminate out-of-date or inefficient assets.

Levi Strauss & Co. doesn't make jeans; its four core values are "empathy, originality, integrity and courage." What? Levi Strauss doesn't make jeans? That's right, it orchestrates a world-wide value system where specialists deal with the yarn spinning, cutting and dying, and sewing. What then does Levi Strauss, in fact, do? It's a brand manager, and one of the very best in the world at that. In its own words, "People love our clothes and trust our company. We will market the most appealing and widely worn casual clothing in the world. We will clothe the world." Why there's nary a mention of manufacturing jeans at Levi Strauss' Values and Vision page at its Web site.

Organizational innovation is about building relationships

with trading partners to form end-to-end value delivery systems, where each trading partner brings its super-specialized resources to the table, thereby optimizing each component in the system. Companies like Levi Strauss must, like a symphony conductor, orchestrate the overall system. Because the company closest to the end customer is in the lead position to determine what customers want, when and where, the well-known companies of the future are likely to be brand managers, perhaps with incredibly small numbers of employees. The no-name companies thrive by being essential participants in the value delivery systems of the brand managers. We've all heard of Hewlett-Packard, but how well known is their key partner, Flextronics in Singapore? Flextronics is a vital, though external, component of HP's organization.

Supply-side Innovation. "In the early 1500s, Italian Renaissance sculptor, painter, architect, and poet Michelangelo organized what may have been the first truly virtual company. He developed a network of trusted suppliers, artists, and stone masons to supply the materials he needed for his work. The comprehensive records he kept for his projects detail the excellent guidance he provided his vendors and his careful monitoring of quality and costs."[24]

In today's global economy, companies scour the world to procure lowest cost resources. There's certainly nothing new about that. Where supply-side innovation kicks in comes in terms of managing a dynamic web of suppliers, or to state it otherwise, to manage multiple supply chains, simultaneously. Individual supply chains may be enacted for just a few customers, or even one customer. Dell manages 30 tier-1 and 400 tier-2 suppliers scattered across the globe in order to maintain multiple supply chains tailored to corporate buyers and consumers, for both its computer and consumer electronics products.

Zara, the Spanish high-fashion retailer, blends supply chains incorporating local vendors with higher cost and fast response time, with lower cost but poor response time suppliers in Eastern Europe and elsewhere to get the best of both worlds. While other high-fashion retailers spend weeks or months waiting for low-cost suppliers scattered from China to Uruguay, Zara needs three weeks for new product development, compared to the nine month industry average, and launches around 10,000 new designs each year. Timing is everything in the world of fashion, and to meet its timing requirements, Zara innovates by making multiple supply chains dance to the tune of high fashion.

Core-competency Innovation. Over the past few decades of downsizing, rightsizing and outsourcing, the one thing a company still holds dear is its "core competency." While handling payrolls is certainly not a core competency, and can be outsourced to a company like ADP, determining exactly what is "core" is increasingly being questioned. Take "design" as a core competency for an auto manufacturer. Mercedes-Benz didn't design its Smart Car, the Swiss watch maker, Swatch did.

What could be considered more core than research and development (R&D)? It is estimated that the U.S. medical device and diagnostics industry currently outsources more than $300 million in R&D.[25] In Taipei, Quanta Computer's ability to *design* and build new laptops from scratch has helped it gain a 25 percent share of all laptops sold in the United States, including brand named notebooks from Apple, HP, and IBM.[26] Henry William Chesbrough writes in his book, *Open Innovation,* "It's a plain fact: regardless of how smart, creative, and innovative your organization is, there are more smart, creative, and innovative people outside your organization than inside." Thus the great research departments at companies like GE's first industrial research lab in the U.S. (born in the carriage barn in Charles Steinmetz's backyard), Bell Labs, IBM Thomas J. Watson Research Center, and Xerox's PARC are moving from owning innovation inside their four walls, and moving to connecting to research done outside their *Not Invented Here (NIH)* cultures (a term used to describe a persistent corporate or institutional culture that avoids using previously performed research or knowledge because the research and developed knowledge was not originally executed in-house). They are reinventing invention by moving from creating the dots, to connecting the dots.

Could further outsourcing of a company's core competencies lead to a *jobless* company, perhaps a company with only a CEO and a small army of patent attorneys (oops, those too could be outsourced)? While the future, hopefully, won't be that pronounced, aggressive companies are finding ways to innovate at their very core to gain competitive advantage.

Sell-side Innovation. Getting a company's offerings to market requires a blend of channels of distribution. When selling through established industry channels, brand strength is key. For example, Procter and Gamble sells a lot of stuff through the mother of all channel masters, Wal-Mart, and if it weren't for its "killer brands" such as Tide, Old Spice, Mr. Clean, and now its recently acquired Gillette razors, Duracell, Braun and Oral-B brands, P&G's already razor thin margins would be squeezed to near zero.

Branding creates demand-pull, and allows trusted brands to demand a premium, even after running through the gauntlet of tight-fisted Wal-Mart buyers. Today, the Internet has created a new source of channel strategy, and more and more companies are now able to reach out to end customers directly. This does not, however, simply eliminate established channels of distribution or intermediaries. Already, notions such as "disintermediation" of value chains have been met with notions of "antidisintermediation." In 1999, Home Depot, in a letter to more than 1,000 vendors including Black & Decker, Scotts, and General Electric, said it may hesitate to do business with suppliers that also market their products online because they would then become competitors. Home Depot said it would prefer to partner with them on selling via the Internet.

Achieving sell-side innovation requires getting closer to your customers, building strong brands, and seeking new channels of distribution, sometime even through your competitors. Fruit of the Loom Activewear's Web site used to sell competitive Hanes products in order to provide a full line of products to T-shirt silk screeners across America, and Virgin Mobil cut a "coopetition" deal with Sprint PCS, making Virgin the 10th largest cell phone provider in the U.S.A. without erecting even one tower. Wal-Mart already has more than a foot in the door in the banking industry by forging alliances with MoneyGram International and SunTrust Banks, making it possible to provide low-priced money orders and wire transfers. Bank branches operated by partners now do business in nearly 1,000 of its super centers. SunTrust is beta testing almost 45 bank branches in Wal-Mart stores called "Wal-Mart Money Center by SunTrust," and expects to have 100 of them by 2006.

Another emerging strategy on the sell-side of companies is that of reaching the underserved segments of markets, that is, creating entirely new markets where none existed before—and to stay below the radar of incumbents in those markets if possible (we'll talk more about this in *Extreme Specialization*).

Product and Service Innovation. Whether a company's offerings are either products or services, innovation is a matter of getting close to a company's customers, so close that it can identify unarticulated or unmet needs. As reported in Business Week, "When GE's medical division installed a vast array of high-tech equipment for a new digital heart hospital in Tampa, not only did GE execs offer the usual equipment and services, they helped build a system around technology GE is developing that isn't even on the market yet. Hospital execs also got advice on leadership development, workplace design, and coordination with other units of GE to help build the facility. The contract will also run up to seven years, vs. the usual one to five years for normal pacts. Other bidders didn't come close in trying to forge a strategic partnership, says COO Brigitte Shaw, adding: 'We don't have the intellectual capital and resources to make this happen on our own.'"[27] When you're at that level of getting close to the customer, that's how you stay ahead. You fuse with the customer, you and the customer become one.

For years Procter and Gamble was the king consumer goods manufacturing. But in 2000, thanks to margin pressures from the likes of Wal-Mart, P&G had to transform itself from a stale brand manager to an innovator. As *Business Week* reported, "Before A. G. Lafley took over as CEO in 2000, P&G's volume growth was basically flat. The company cared more about how its products functioned than it did about how customers felt about them. 'P&G had the best chemical engineering and marketing operations in the country,' says Patrick Whitney, director of the Institute of Design at Illinois Institute of Technology. 'It didn't care about the user experience.' P&G could tell retailers to stock eight kinds of Crest, and they did. As power shifted to big retailers, P&G couldn't do that. 'It had to create new products, and to do that, P&G had to get closer to the consumer,' says Whitney. Lafley turned to design. Even as P&G began laying off thousands of top executives, middle managers, scientists, and others, it quadrupled its design staff. For the first time it hired a legion of designers who had worked at other companies and in other industries. This changed P&G's entire innovation process, making it consumer-centric rather than driven by new technology."

What we are seeing is the evolution of traditional, inside-out, R&D-based product innovation to an outside-in approach to innovation that starts with customers. That evolution started with products, then moved to product services, and, as we'll discuss later in this book, on to "experiences." Because consumers want solutions, not products (they really want a hole, not a drill), smart companies have transformed from just selling products to selling product services. General Motors no longer just sells cars; it sells *a safer, easier and more productive ride* with its OnStar technology and services. GE has grown from a product-based company into a services company that also makes great products. Seventy percent of GE's revenue comes from services and, increasingly, from product services. Two decades ago, when Jack Welch took the helm, only fifteen percent of GE's revenues came from services.[28]

Starbucks is the poster child of the emerging "experience economy." Just as GE evolved from a product-based to product-services company, the staying power of companies will be measured by their ability to go beyond delivering products and services, and on to delivering innovative experiences that people incorporate into their lifestyles.

Innovating Innovation Itself. Returning to Business

Week's Bruce Nussbaum, "There is, in fact, a whole new generation of innovation gurus. They are not the superstars of the '90s, such as Clayton Christensen, who focused on what might be called macro-innovation—the impact of big, unexpected new technologies on companies. The new gurus focus more on micro-innovation—teaching companies how to connect with their customers' emotions, linking research and development labs to consumer needs, recalibrating employee incentives to emphasize creativity, constructing maps showing opportunities for innovation."

But there's more to innovating innovation; it's about innovation as a *systematic and repeatable business process.* The man who just might turn out to be the Edwards Demming of 21st century innovation, Howard Smith, CTO of CSC's Innovation Center of Excellence in Europe, thinks business innovation is really about *process.* Where Demming brought process to the quality movement, Smith goes beyond the notions of creativity, invention and design to bring a rigorous problem-solving process to innovation. "Reflecting on the invention of the Alto personal office computer, author, consultant and former Director at Xerox PARC labs, John Seely Brown observes that 'as much, if not more, creativity goes into the implementation part of the innovation as into the invention itself.' In this respect, Xerox, the inventor, failed as an innovator, leaving billions in profits for Apple and Microsoft. Creativity, invention, design and business innovation are often confused."

Smith explains, "Innovation is a holistic process involving the entire organization of a commercial enterprise, whereas invention is a discrete event, typically performed by specialist individuals or very small teams. Innovation requires multi-disciplinary teams and is a complete lifecycle process. Creativity and design are necessary, but insufficient. In this sense, IDEO's [one of the world's great design firms] design innovations are, like every other element in the *operating system for innovation,* a part of the mix. Yet in a world of product abundance, mass-customization and extraordinary high expectations when consumers interact with public or private services or business people deal with suppliers, IDEO's core competence is no doubt a vital ingredient. Their design process turns genuine inventions into useable, interesting and beautiful products and services, rendering them acceptable to commercialization. And what IDEO produces must be relevant to markets, and the timing of the release of those innovations to markets is critical, as Christensen has taught us. Yet just as we must move beyond Christensen's management frameworks if we are to understand the sources of innovation and the critical role of problem solving, so too must we move beyond IDEO's design innovation if we are to understand the full extent of what innovation is. Seen as the creator of new value, innovation isn't hit-or-miss, trial-and-error lateral thinking, but a repeatable process. What is innovative about innovation today is the realization that it can be achieved systematically, and that the innovator is an obsessive *problem solver.*"

To put teeth into his approach of business innovation as problem solving, Smith goes way beyond the many techniques and methods most often associated with innovation, "But if you thought you had heard about all the best-practice acronyms and trends out there, think again. To the current plethora of strategies for adaptation and survival is now added something that may be a way of thinking, a set of tools, a methodology, a process, a theory or even possibly a deep science, but which may be gradually shaping up as 'the next

big thing.' It's called TRIZ, pronounced 'trees' and is an acronym for the Russian words that translate as 'The Theory of
Inventive Problem Solving.' Its systematic approach to innovation is the antisepsis of unreliable, hit and miss, trial and
error, psychological means of lateral thinking. Its scientific,
repeatable, procedural and algorithmic processes surprise all
who first encounter them. Sound like magic?

"After just one TRIZ workshop, engineers at National
Semiconductor modified a machine that tests integrated cir-
cuits (ICs) that had gobbled up $76,000 in the previous five
months of trial and error. Within a week, TRIZ-based software responded with 40 directions in which the engineers
could investigate a solution. The most promising idea was the
replacement of frail IC contacts with an elastomer, reducing
the physical impact to IC leads during insertion. The consen-
sus among the engineers working on the problem at the time
was that, without guidance from TRIZ, the project would still
have been hunting for a solution. Other companies have had
similar experiences.

"As globalization advances and companies see fewer opportunities for growth, the clamor for invention and innovation—proxies for 'economic value'—will inexorably rise. Innovation poster-child GE redid a twenty three year old slogan
called, 'We bring good things to life,' and replaced it with a
slogan called, 'Imagination at work.' The firm includes a creative drawing tool on its Web home page. By contrast, FedEx
is almost dull. Its core competence in logistics implies supply-
chain efficiency and reliability. Those qualities define the
FedEx 'identity' business process.

"Is FedEx less innovative than GE? Not necessarily. What
do GE and FedEx have in common? Both are obsessive
problem solvers.

"Companies do more than perfect the known and optimize for efficiency. Glib use of the terms 'creativity' or 'innovation' means little if relevant problems are not being solved. Innovative firms develop an ability to solve problems that remove barriers to greater economic value. Whether an engineer is figuring out why an industrial process won't start, or a call centre operator is re-designing support processes to avoid answering similar problems over and over again, both are solving problems and each requires methodology and in-context expertise. At the macro level, numerous elements are involved: a learning environment, creative thinking tools, design flair, engineering skill, scientific method, enabling work practices, an amenable culture, specific organizational structures, supportive management frameworks, numerous business processes, information systems, market strategy, inventive and predictive algorithms. At the micro level it comes down to the individual employees, their talent, qualifications and knowledge."

TAKEAWAY: Recognizing innovation as a systematic business process is far more important than just creating "an innovation," for if a company is to lead, it must set the "pace of innovation" (see also *The Pace of Innovation* later in this book). To become a serial innovator, a company will need to view innovation as an ongoing process of problem solving that spans all six dimensions of business innovation.

3. Extreme Individuals

Knowledge work no longer requires corralling specialists into corporate labs such as IBM's vintage Thomas J. Watson Research Center or GE's venerable Thomas Edison research labs in New York. It also means that individuals can be set free of the bonds of corporate indenture.

Even in the complex world of advanced information technology, it is often the work of one or a few researchers that leads to a breakthrough, not some huge lab. For example, Google, Inc. began as a research project in early 1996 by two individuals, Larry Page and Sergey Brin, Ph.D. students at Stanford University. They developed the idea that a search engine based on the analysis of the relationships between Web sites would produce improved results over the basic techniques then in use. Convinced that the pages with the most links to them from other highly relevant Web pages must be the most relevant pages associated with the search, Page and Brin laid the foundation for their "page-ranked" search engine.

The domain, google.com, was registered in September, 1997, and then they incorporated in September, 1998 at a friend's garage in Menlo Park, California. Google's initial public offering took place in August, 2004 with 19,605,052 shares offered at a price of $85 per share. The sale raised $1.67 billion, and generated a market capitalization of more than $23 billion. Many of Google's employees became instant paper millionaires. In November, 2005, with share prices hovering around $382, Google was valued at $111.7 billion, making it the world's biggest media company by stock market value, surpassing Time Warner ($80.8 billion market cap). Not bad, for a business started by two young individuals.

Returning from cyberspace, in August 2005, gasoline prices in the U.S. were marching toward $4.00 a gallon and crude oil had hit a record $70+ per barrel. Every penny increase in gasoline prices means that U.S. consumers pay about $139 billion extra at the pump each year.

While politicians and automakers say a car that can free the U.S. from its reliance on foreign oil is years or even decades away, Californian Ron Gremban, says such a car is parked in his garage. It looks like a typical Toyota Prius hybrid, but in the trunk sits an 80-miles-per-gallon secret: 18 brick-sized batteries that let him store extra power by plugging the car into a wall outlet at his home—for about a quarter. Meanwhile, University of California professor Andy Frank, has built a plug-in hybrid that gets up to 250 mpg. Frank believes automakers could mass-produce them by adding just $6,000 to each vehicle's price tag.

Even Toyota, the company that has spent millions leading the race for hybrid technology, and whose officials initially frowned on people altering their cars, now say they may be able to learn from such "hot rod" individuals. Don't be surprised if Ron Gremban or Andy Frank become household names in the auto industry. That's simply the nature of "knowledge as capital."

In John Naisbitt's 1994 book, *Global Paradox*, the central idea is that *the bigger the world economy, the more powerful its smallest players.* Naisbitt explains that the hugeness of companies, like IBM and General Motors, was fine when economies of scale were needed, but goes on to assert that hugeness leads to innovation-stifling bureaucracies. He prescribed that these unwieldy monoliths restyle themselves into networks of entrepreneurs, and writes that "entrepreneurs—individuals—are creating the huge global economy."

Perhaps one of the clearest examples of empowering individuals comes from the publishing industry, an industry shrouded in mystery for the ordinary person. "Congratulations! You're a published author." That's *not* what most aspiring authors hear after preparing long and elaborate book proposals for traditional publishers. But Canadian entrepreneur Bob Young, the founder of Red Hat, the Linux software company that has mounted a serious challenge to Microsoft, has turned the publishing industry upside down and inside out, handing complete control of the entire process to the individual. His Lulu.com site offers all the digital ingredients for anyone to become a published author. By totally demystifying the publishing business, Lulu gives budding writers, photographers and musicians the chance to get their works published, and not one dime moves unless triggered by a sale.

Many works are rejected by regular publishers because they do not think many copies of a title will be sold, and the cost for them of going into production cannot be justified. Not so with Lulu. Thanks to on-demand printing, if an author makes money, Lulu makes money. If the author produces a dud, no one makes money, but there aren't warehouses of books to throw in to the trash bin, thus no one loses money. Basic services on Lulu are free, although there is a fee to be listed on Amazon and Barnes & Noble Booksellers. There also is a cost for distribution services, which makes it easier to sell books in stores and elsewhere. There's an e-book publishing option, too. In short, Lulu covers the entire publishing industry, from content creation to serving multiple channels of distribution. Anyone can publish, sell and buy any and all things digital—books, music, comics, photographs, and movies. Lulu simply provides the tools that leave control of content in the hands of the individuals who create the content. Because Lulu is a technology company, not a traditional publisher, there is no set-up fee and no minimum order to publish and sell on Lulu.com. Lulu manages the online business, including printing, delivery and customer service. Authors set their own royalties for each piece of content, and at the end of each quarter, Lulu mails a check for the royalties. Lulu makes a small percentage from each transaction, which means that it only makes money if its authors succeed in selling their works. Okay, the name "Lulu" is dippy, an old-fashioned term for a remarkable person, object or idea. And quite frankly, that's exactly what Lulu, the company, is. Think of it as an open marketplace for digital content—the Web's version of a fresh air market.

Companies like eBay, Google, Lulu, and Skype are building their businesses on the "individual empowerment" model. In essence they have built "digital platforms" around which individuals are disrupting established industries. Okay, now an individual can become a published author, but how about an individual becoming a phone company?

With globalization on the rise, there is a big market for international cell phone calls, and a little known company, iSkoot, is creating a really unique offering in that market. It is like VOIP on steroids, and could commoditize the wireless international cell phone industry. The iSkoot founder, Jacob Guedalia, said his vision was to "enable the individual to become his own long-distance carrier" by routing calls over a home or office computer connection, instead of AT&T or Sprint. Headquartered in Cambridge, Mass., iSkoot is dedicated to becoming a leader in enabling mobile Internet telephony. The company is leveraging Skype's ecosystem of over 51 million subscribers to provide services and technology to disrupt the international wireless industry.

Thanks to Skype making its software code available to other technology developers to build new services and products that run over Skype, Guedalia said, "We can take the voice-over-Internet revolution, which until now has really been confined to the personal computer, and bring it to the mobile world." For a $10-a-year software fee, iSkoot lets people make international calls to other Skype users for noth-

ing more than the price of local air time for the link from
their cell phones to their broadband-connected home computers. Stated another way, iSkoot empowers individuals to
become their own international telephone carriers.

So powerful is the combination that, according to a
Reuters report, China Telecom is starting to block Skype ser-
vice in Shenzhen, an affluent southern city of China. Local
Chinese media report that China Telecom has plans to even-
tually block the service throughout its coverage area nation-
wide. Could this have something to do with the fact that
China Telecom charges close to $1 per minute for calls to
United States and Europe while Skype is free?

TAKEAWAY: John Naisbitt's 1994 proclamation that *the
bigger the world economy, the more powerful its smallest players,* has
been validated with the ability of special individuals to connect to anyone or any company, and visa versa. The individual is now a powerful source of competitive advantage: for
example, consider the two college students who started
Google, a company whose market capitalization of $111.7
billion in November, 2005 surpassed even mighty Time Warner ($80.8 billion).

4. Extreme Customization[29]

The customer has become the dictator, thanks to advances
in technology and the Internet. Mass production is giving way
to various forms of "mass customization" such as build-to-
order, make-to-demand, and "customerization" where,
mostly digital products like Apple's iTunes, are customized by
the consumer. Customers are forcing enterprises to continuously raise the bar on individualization. Customers want
goods and services to be tailored to their individual needs, in
a real-time manner, with mass production prices. Customers

also want to be involved in the design of these good and services. The customer wants its supplier to create a porous and transparent business process, and wants to be involved in the full lifecycle of process activities, from initial selection and configuration of a product or service, all the way through to its usage and ultimate disposal.

While customized computers, electronics, and apparel are innovations of the past, forward looking companies are racing ahead to new frontiers of customization. For example, the British insurer Norwich Union is revolutionizing car insurance by creating "Pay As You Drive" car insurance policy. By placing GPS receivers in the trunks, data from the devices will be used to adjust premiums month to month based on how much and how a customer drives. Customers therefore can control monthly insurance premiums by driving safely. Norwich Union says customers will see a savings of up to 30% a year.

Even highway tolls are being customized. Intelligent transportation systems are being created by IBM to allow drivers to pay variable tolls based on their status: city official, ambulance, commuter, taxi, and so on.

Stylingcard AG, a Zurich based company, is creating a customization "platform" where customers, retailers and manufacturers can do business. Think of it as an eBay for customization. Stylingcard creates a virtual twin for each participating customer. The virtual twin is a digital representation of the customer based on the collection and presentation of a detailed personal profile. The personal profile is a combination of high quality 3-D scanning data and a structured analysis of personal requirements and wishes. The entire data constitutes the virtual twin. Each customer is owner of his own data, and can update the virtual twin as desired.

The Stylingcard platform connects customers, retailers and manufacturers. Customers can choose products like clothes, shoes, jewelry, eye-glasses, and much more based on their profiles, giving retailers the opportunities to offer a much larger range of customized products and services. Manufacturers can receive electronically readable orders, based on 100% transparent data that drives custom manufacturing.

Customization doesn't always imply an individualized, make-to-order business model. Build-to-order, by definition, means fulfillment of a single custom order, generally by assembling pre-fabricated parts into various combinations based on information supplied by configuring the desired product features. In contrast, the *make-to-demand* business model is a source of competitive advantage that supersedes the forecast-buy-sell model, the supply-push model of the past, with a radically streamlined demand-pull model of business. At heart of the make-to-demand model is the availability of real-time demand data. For example, potato chips aren't made for individual customers, but highly customized supply chains are needed to fulfill the specific needs for specific stores at specific times. This is because in the consumer goods markets, up to 30% of merchandise categories, such as potato chips, are sold during promotions.

Make-to-demand is a broader concept than the build-to-order process. Going forward, build-to-order will be just one fulfillment component of the more strategic vision of make-to-demand, where companies use sense and respond capabilities built on Internet connectivity, and use marketing and innovation to actually shape demand.

TAKEAWAY: Thanks to manufacturing techniques such as the Toyota Production System, mass production has given way to mass customization. Make-to-order and make-to-demand business models are now fundamental to the ability to compete.

5. Extreme Business Processes[30]

Business process collaboration is one counter measure against rapid change. Process collaboration can take several forms: sharing or outsourcing back office operations; tangible and intangible asset sharing; and collaborative research and marketing. The virtues of process collaboration are clear—rapid innovation, effectiveness and efficiency.

Process interaction between and among actors in the value chain is the enabler of inter-company operations. As shown below, inter-company process integration can be measured at three levels: simple data handoffs, process handoffs and shared real-time processes.

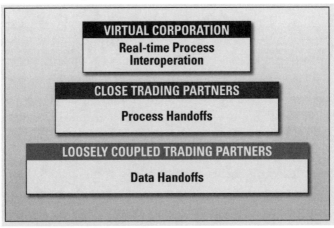

Inter-enterprise Process Integration Levels

Simple data handoffs represent a level of integration that's simply a digital media replacement for paper shuffling (faxes or documents sent through the mail). At the next level, digital transactions trigger the processes in the systems of other par-

ticipants. For example, an order processing system of a retailer may trigger inventory status processes within a supplier's system—the processes in the transaction are aligned
via process handoffs. At the highest level of inter-enterprise
process integration, processes are jointly owned and interop-
erate in real-time. The user of such systems cannot tell which
sub-processes are running on whose internal systems—the
user is just interacting with "the system." Full process integration gives each player in a value chain full access to information and services, both up and downstream. For example customer information is available throughout the value chain,
not just to the seller. Such information sharing can allow each
participant in the value chain to optimize its performance in
real time.

As globalization continues, a combination of these three
process arrangements needs to be supported simultaneously.
Players in a value chain will have differing technological capabilities and readiness for process sharing. For example, a
mom 'n pop specialty manufacturer of components may not
have a computer but can participate in a value chain by fax,
just like in the traditional world of commerce. Others in the
same value chain may participate only by email, while yet
other participants are connected in real time, 7x24.

Sharing Back Office Operations. Avendra, the hospitality industry's leading procurement services company was initially
setup by Hyatt Hotels Corporation, Marriott International,
ClubCorp USA, Fairmont Hotels & Resorts and Interconti-
nental Hotels Group. Today it offers procurement services to
several hotel chains. Avendra collaborates with these hotel
chains to provide them procurement services—a totally
unique concept and a very innovative idea in the industry.
Avendra crafts customized procurement processes for each

of its clients—recognizing their need for individuality—yet leverages its buying power and supply chain expertise to drive value to its customers.

Avendra works deep in the supply chain, going beyond the distributor to negotiate attractive pricing with manufacturers and sometimes raw materials suppliers. Avendra offers its customers a wide range of flexible purchasing solutions. Its purchasing programs are comprised of over 900 suppliers, offering significant cost savings and enhanced service levels. Further, Avendra offers its clients a wide range of specialized knowledge services such as quality assurance and operational audits, best practices consulting, specification development, purchasing information and more to help customers maximize their procurement operations.

The suppliers of products and services to Avendra's platform enjoy the benefits of increased access to hospitality customers, enhanced customer service through better reporting and real-time information access, standardized and simplified business processes, increased sales volume potential, and heightened market exposure through Avendra's national marketing campaigns.

Avendra is essentially a knowledge broker in the hospitality industry. Avendra's success depends on a deep understanding of its industry, economics and the requirements of both its clients and suppliers. Basically, Avendra is a *process orchestrator* and has created a process network that provides value to all participants. Avendra uses its operational information to give its suppliers in-depth feedback, which ensures continuous product and service improvement. The broad knowledge of the supply chain enables Avendra to quickly tailor its supply chain to meet each customer's changing needs. Such extreme process collaboration results in economies of scale, leveraged buying opportunities, and improved knowledge for procuring products and services for all of Avendra's customers. The company has grown to nearly $2 billion in purchasing volume from the time it was founded in 2001, despite the hospitality industry recession after 9/11. In fact, Avendra and Fairmont Hotels & Resorts (a hotelier with 83 hotels in eight countries) were honored with the "Most Innovative Relationship" award by the Outsourcing Center and Forbes Magazine. The award honors the six most outstanding outsourcing relationships each year.

Back-office outsourcing is a cornerstone of the growing globalization trend. The Indian Business Process Outsourcing (BPO) industry grew 40%, to $5.8 billion, in 2004, and is expected to hit $64 billion and employ 3 million people in 2012, according to a Nasscom/KPMG study. India won't be able to reach its BPO goals by only offering cheap labor. That's why one Indian company, Wipro, is adopting the management practices from the world-famous Toyota production system, and applying Toyota's quality improvement lessons to the services Wipro provides—from smart and lean manufacturing to smart and lean services. Wipro has made the book, *The Toyota Way,* mandatory reading, and don't be surprised if *The Wipro Way,* isn't a future management best seller on how to establish a service culture capable of delivering successful outcomes that exceed customers' expectations.

After returning from delivering a professional class on BPM for Wipro in Bangalore, Mark McGregor, senior coach at the Business Process Management Group in the U.K., wrote, "I have to say that I have never come across a group of such intelligent and smart people so willing to learn and have their existing practices and beliefs challenged."[1]

It's precisely that attitude that will surely drive success in the Indian BPO industry. While China may be the workshop of the world (capitalizing on 9-cent per hour factory labor), India may well become the world's back office.

Sharing Tangible and Intangible Assets. Process collaboration has become strategic, and companies that are unprepared for this new form of business interaction will struggle. Forward looking companies are collaborating and outsourcing even their "core processes," like R&D, engineering and financial management.

The electronics sector is furthest down the road, but other industries are watching and following. The Asian manufacturers of the 1980s, and the PC designers and assemblers of the 1990s are constantly moving up the value chain and leveraging experience across product and industry segments. More and more players are jumping into the fray with products that, until recently, only giants like Sony, Sharp and Panasonic could produce. Dell, HP, and a variety of no-name players are now hopping on the consumer-electronics bandwagon. This superheated competition and the relentless demands for better, faster and cheaper products and services in the consumer electronics market are constantly reducing the "time to commoditization" for all products—PDA's, digital cameras, mobile phones, PCs, network equipment, and so on.

To stay ahead of the cycle of rapid commoditization and margin decline, companies must get innovative products out of the door fast, and must set the pace of innovation thereafter, as competitors are sure to catch up with any given innovation. Sometimes the innovation race is so intense, it's like a

---

[1] Mark also took advantage of the low-cost, high-quality Indian dental care, and had £500 worth of treatment for only £50 during his stay!

rapper's endless pursuit of *bling* (anything shiny and worth a good amount of money).

It is no longer feasible or practical for companies to own the entire array of assets needed to develop an innovative product or service. Companies need to collaborate with a global network of super-specialized partners to churn out innovative products and stay ahead of competition. The only practical way they can do that is through sophisticated business-to-business interactions made possible by a new form of IT called business process management (BPM).

Let's see what one super-specialized company does in this new digital, process-powered world of strategic alliances. Working behind the scenes for companies like Microsoft, Sun, Nortel, Xerox, HP, Motorola, Ericsson, and Sony, is Flextronics, a Singaporean contract manufacturer that has become "the biggest tech company you've never heard of." From its modest beginnings in 1990, Flextronics has become a global giant of tech manufacturing and assembly, product design and testing. With $15.9 billion in annual revenues and 95,000 employees, it is larger than many of its customers.

The popular products the company makes are everywhere: all of Microsoft's Xbox game consoles, most of Hewlett-Packard's inkjet printers, all of Xerox's desktop copiers, all of Sony Ericsson's cell phones, and much of Nortel's telecommunications equipment ($2 billion). All these products have "*Flextronics Inside*," but strict confidentiality agreements with its customers prevent Flextronic's from talking openly.

Based on what services (design, manufacturing, assembly, testing, or all of these) the customer wants, Flextronics enables its customer's processes to collaborate with its own processes in real time. This process collaboration makes Flextronics a virtual extension of its customers' businesses.

For the production of Xbox, Microsoft was able to collaborate with Flextronic's manufacturing processes in real time and maintain complete visibility and control of the entire production process. Microsoft wanted to get the Xbox out before the Holiday shopping season of 2001—so quality, cost and time-to-market were all critical. According to Todd Holmdahl, general manager for Xbox hardware, "These [process] tools give us the ability to view all inventory positions, including work in progress, warehouse inventories, vendor-managed inventory, and inventory levels on hand at suppliers. We also have the ability to see real-time production outputs, by factory, by SKU (stock keeping unit), by line."

Sun Microsystems is a virtual manufacturer as a result of process collaboration. Sun takes orders from customers, configures systems, and then hands the orders off to external manufacturing partners for production and shipment. The only part of the order Sun touches directly is the information. Sun uses an assortment of suppliers, including Flextronics.

Flextronics has created intangible assets—R&D, product lifecycle management processes and organization structures to enable its customers to plug into its work processes. Behind the intangible assets are Flextronics' tangible assets. Flextronics has a network of physical facilities in 32 countries and five continents. This global presence provides customers with complete design, engineering, and manufacturing resources that are vertically integrated with tangible component capabilities to optimize their operations by lowering their costs and reducing their time to market. Flextronics is thriving because it has created the tangible resource balance for process collaboration. Flextronics' acquisition of Hughes Software and Frog Design Inc. signals that Flextronics wants to become a one stop, soup-to-nuts developer of electronics and tech equipment.

Other firms in the consumer electronic space, like Compal, HTC, and Quanta, all in Taiwan, are climbing up the innovation chain. Some critics say that companies that collaborate with networks of partners on everything from design, software, and manufacturing, risk becoming irrelevant and losing sustainable competitive advantage. *BusinessWeek* ran an article in March 2005 titled "Outsourcing Innovation," saying companies might be going too far in farming out R&D to cut costs and get products to the markets faster. Truth be known, companies have a tough balancing act ahead as they seek to innovate through alliances, while retaining their proprietary advantages. In many cases this will lead to the continued rise of patent filings, and the increasing use of massive advertising budgets and public relations campaigns by what some are already calling the "branding bullies." On the other hand, innovative small companies will stay under the radar of the huge transnational corporations, and focus their offerings on the underserved segments of markets, or use "unbranding" and "no logo" techniques (American Apparel in the U.S. and Muji in Japan) to appeal to those fed up with in-your-face brands.

In summary, business process collaboration is at the heart of creating 21st century "killer value chains." All is changed as new forms of supply chains, and even core-competency webs, are bubbling up across the globe.

TAKEAWAY: Companies must now compete with their business processes—the way work gets done, *how* they *do* what they do. New process management tools and techniques enable bewildering new possibilities for the way work gets done, where it gets done, by whom and for whom. Dell, the mighty computer company, sells a commodity, yet is the envy of its industry by innovating with its business processes.

6. Extreme Teams

In a wired world, the possibilities for assembling, then disbanding, geographically scattered project teams are almost endless. A growing numbers of companies are relying on electronically connected virtual teams to get things done. Armed with digital collaboration tools and techniques, some have already gone so far as to reinvent themselves as "virtual companies," like Decathlon Systems, a 30-employee, software firm in Colorado that re-engineered its entire organization. Readily available collaboration technologies, including e-mail, group calendaring and scheduling, group resource management, cooperative document editing, and personal information management tools have been enough to transform the company. Before reengineering itself, all Decathlon employees worked in one 6,000 square foot office. Now each and every Decathlon staff member telecommutes.

Similarly, Nissan Motor Co., expects to save at least $135 million over the next few years, and to bring vehicles to market quicker, because its technology infrastructure upgrade is vastly facilitating global collaboration. And Bullivant, Houser, Bailey, Pendergrass & Hoffman, a Portland law firm, not only uses technology-enabled collaboration to save its clients legal fees, but also to extend its organization to include its clients. Digital collaboration lets clients examine documents in the working file or database, saving up to 20 percent of the firm's clerical costs.

In time, the primary work unit in the enterprise is likely to be a virtual, matrixed team, composed of diverse competencies, knowledge and capabilities, with traditional hierarchical structures replaced by teams assembled to tackle specific tasks. In this new scenario, and to paraphrase Shakespeare, "All the world's a project. And all the men and systems merely play their roles; They have their exits and their entrances." Indeed, the ability to model and implement "roles" digitally is the key to next generation collaboration support technologies.

"Connect and collaborate" is the future for forming high performance teams, but it's not all that easy, and a new generation of collaboration tools will be needed.

Assisting organizations to manage those exit and entrance points in typical collaborations is a new breed of business technology, the Human Interaction Management System—*workware* technology that animates human work and collaboration in much the way software animates computer hardware. While business executives don't want more and more software, they know they need workware, for they know how complex their business operations have become. This is precisely the kind of business technology needed for teams scattered across the globe to work together effectively. Although just emerging as a business technology, and only catching the eyes of early adopters, the Human Interaction Management System could soon become as prevalent as email is today.

Furthermore, those many organizations building new models for success around the work of teams, whose members are scattered across multiple geographic locations, are coming to realize leadership of a virtual project team is an art in itself. When it comes to the complexities of getting individuals in vastly dispersed locations to function as a cohesive unit, Hollywood—that master of reinvention—has been showing the way for decades.

From the turn of the 19th century through to the mid-1940s, Hollywood was pretty much a self-contained world of mini-moguls running film production "factory lines" and controlling everything, including the lives of workers, stars, directors and writers. Five major studios totally dominated the business of making movies: administering production, distribution and exhibition through their own chains of theaters, and binding actors and directors with onerous and exclusive contracts of as much as seven years duration. Studios had their own nurseries, schools, police forces and fire stations. The moguls had the mindset of dictators the world over, and it was wise to think like them and behave according to their dictates if you wanted to secure your film career.

With the so-called "Studio Model" beginning to unravel in 1938 in face of antitrust and other lawsuits, Hollywood teetered close to extinction until it did the one thing that Hollywood has excelled at since its inception. It reinvented itself. Recognizing the need to maintain intellectual capital while breaking free of the legislative tethers that were increasingly containing them, the studios chose to adopt what is now known as the "Hollywood Model," under which nearly all production was outsourced.

Most people working in Hollywood have always been what today are described as knowledge workers, from cameramen to editors to musicians. All are creative and capable of creating or being part of the creation of new copyright. The group-think fostered by the Studio Model did its level best to stifle such creativity. But now, under the new Hollywood Model, the studios leave the production of films (and much of the financial risk) primarily to outside independent producers. Once financing is found for a film, the producer hires a production manager and together they assemble the film crew. Each crew member is hired for his or her specialized skills, and crew members and their skills are assembled or dropped out as needs dictate. When the production is wrapped up, most crew members are released, and post-production begins with a skeleton crew, which is also hired only when needed.

The typical duration of this new breed of film production company is barely longer than it takes to make a particular film. Work completed, the team is dissolved. There are no stars or directors under long-term contracts to be automatically used for ongoing productions. Instead specialists come together to work on a project, and then disband. While the model is far from perfect, it has secured the survival of the industry in the face of such extreme disruptive technologies such as the advent of sound, television and color television.

Now Hollywood producers must conquer complex logistics and budgets to create thousands of jobs for occasionally temperamental actors, writers, directors and crew, then find creative ways to market their products all over the world. Hollywood today is a place where "anything is possible," notes Australian producer Hal McElroy, whose credits during 30 years in the film and television industries include Blue Heelers, Picnic at Hanging Rock, The Sum of Us, The Last Wave, Razorback, Water Rats, Murder Call, Return to Eden and the U.S. network success, The Last Frontier, and who has raised tens of millions of dollars for projects during countless trips to Hollywood. Literally anything can be bought or negotiated. It is capitalism in its purest most market-driven form.

Logically, anything Hollywood can do, the rest of industry ought to be able to do as well, or better. Under today's theoretical Hollywood model, capital investment risk can be quarantined by outsourcing production and financing on a project by project basis, putting together a team for a particular task, hiring equipment, offices and talent; then at the end, disbanding the team and closing it down. The results are finite demands, theoretically finite costs and zero holding, carrying, or future costs, meeting head on the challenges of costing and budgeting something that's never been built before. And, aren't these the same challenges companies face when they outsource their supply chains or R&D?

"From the outside, Hollywood and everybody in the industry is perceived to be classically irresponsible and just completely careless, where we simply grab a big bundle of money and run out to the desert and start making things until we run out of money and demand more," McElroy says. "Actually, the whole process is incredibly disciplined. For example in making The Lord of the Rings every single frame of those three films was broken down into its constituent parts, and then individually budgeted and then pre-visualized in the form of storyboards. The series was also recorded with a rough soundtrack, just using guide actors saying the words. Test music was also included, and so they made three films in what are called animatics before they even started producing anything. This approach contained the costs, which is how they were able to make three films for what has been variously described as something like $250 million."

In Hollywood and the television industry today, McElroy says, it is impossible to get the money to make a production unless you've drawn up a budget that may run a hundred pages long, and you've agreed, to the cent, exactly how much the project will cost. The kind of rise and fall clauses found in the construction industry would be totally unacceptable. Certainly there are still occasional cost blow-outs—which naturally make the headlines—but McElroy says that because all production is project financed, and to get that finance the project must first be broken down into constituent parts, the industry is, on the whole, highly disciplined.

Above all, the best producers never lose sight of the fact

that movie-making is, overall, a people business.

Whether it's inside or outside Hollywood, when it comes to managing people, there's a growing need for ditigal tools for supporting dynamic human-to-human interactions. These interactions cannot be preordained or preprogrammed the way computer-to-computer system interactions are. Further, it's the human-driven business processes that are the very heart of all successful business-to-supplier or business-to-customer interactions.

In the groundbreaking book, *Human Interactions,* Keith Harrison-Broninski describes how people really work and how they can be helped to work better. According to Harrison-Broninski, we must ask, "What is involved in amplifying human-driven processes? We need to first understand how to formally describe the human interactions that accomplish work. This should lead us naturally to a better understanding of how to manage those interactions. Then—ideally—we can capture this understanding in a computer system, a Human Interaction Management System."

Human interaction management is not concerned with the individual, detailed tasks of a single worker, such as writing a document, doing a calculation, or giving a presentation. Instead, it concerns the higher-level processes that give work shape and structure as people work together to reach a shared goal. We need to find ways of thinking about human-driven processes that allow the controlled management of change—something that is innate in all work interactions between humans. This way of thinking, just in itself, delivers to the enterprise the ability to regain control of the kind of dynamic, collaborative, geographically diverse activities characterized by the Hollywood Model. However, the techniques of human interaction management, being based on formal principles, provide more than just this. Human interaction management techniques show how to model all human work processes in a way that allows us to support them properly with software. Software support can make it far easier to participate in, measure, and facilitate processes that not only involve multiple players, but also evolve continuously throughout their lifetime—as they do in the messy real world of business.

In the real-time age of globalization, the process-managed enterprise will dominate by implementing radically new means of support for human interactions. Winning companies will deploy innovative information technology tools to manage human-driven processes, capture information deeply personal to each participant, and help people to use this information, both individually and collaboratively. With a new breed of software, the Human Interaction Management System, smart companies will be able to optimize the human-driven processes that are, in the end, their jobs—and the next source of competitive advantage. And, such systems will be as accessible and easy to use as email is today—they will become a natural part of getting work done.

Human interaction management methods and techniques can permit companies to establish a fundamentally human integration (versus machine integration) with their customers, by engaging directly with the human-centered processes for which their products will be used. In the twenty-first century, where customers are bewildered by choice and seek understanding from their suppliers, as well as low price and efficient delivery, such integration will be a necessity. Customers will find suppliers that they trust, engage with them, and stick with them. Anyone can compete in this heady new world—but to keep the customers you gain, you need human interaction management.

After fifty years of computer systems that treat humans simply as data processing engines, we need computer systems that understand and support the complex work humans really carry out, if we are to benefit from an increasing sophisticated business ecosystem. Just consider the last wave of enterprise systems, Customer Relationship Management (CRM). Their 80% failure rate is well known, and it's clear that sales and marketing people were pushed over the top not only by having to get their work done, but also in having to feed and care for these information-processing CRM beasts. Revolt! Even the man most associated with CRM systems, Tom Siebel, pronounced that "CRM is dead." Long live the business processes that actually support customer relationships—and those are human-driven processes.

Bill Gates, in an email prior to Microsoft's 2005 CEO Conference, wrote, "To tackle these challenges [of information overload], information-worker software needs to evolve. It's time to build on the capabilities we have today and create software that helps information workers adapt and thrive in an ever-changing work environment. Now more than ever, competitive advantage comes from the ability to transform ideas into value—through process innovation, strategic insights and customized services. At Microsoft, we believe that the key to helping businesses become more agile and productive in the global economy is to empower individual workers—giving them tools that improve efficiency and enable them to focus on the highest-value work. And a new generation of software is an important ingredient in making this happen. In a new world of work, where collaboration, business intelligence and prioritizing scarce time and attention are critical factors for success, the tools that information workers use must evolve in ways that do not add new complexity for people who already feel the pressure of an 'always-on' world and ever-rising expectations for productivity."[31]

Gates has been serving up his vision of "the new world of work," which he characterizes by inter-company collaboration as a result of the globalization of white-collar work and new forms of government regulation, such as Sarbanes Oxley. Both Gates, and CEO Steve Balmer, at TechEd, indicate that Microsoft intends to beef up its Office suite with human interaction capabilities. An even stronger indication that a new breed of software is in Microsoft's sights is the company's acquisition of Groove Networks, a provider of peer-to-peer "shared spaces." The goal seems clear: incorporate software that helps workers collaborate, search for information sans information overload, and manage information needed for working on ad hoc projects. After all, in the world of today's information workers, life is but a stream of projects. Microsoft seems intent on providing the tools needed to organize human activities around information while, at the same time, taming information overload, taking on information chaos. But is that enough? Not exactly.

It's not enough to organize human activities around information; it must be organized around the work itself.

In the Industrial Age human activities were organized around the assembly line; and in the Information Age human activities are organized around information (the raison d'etre for functional management). In the emerging Process Age, where a company's business processes are key to effectiveness, it's now time to organize human activities around the work itself. That means fusing traditional collaboration and information tools and extending them with a complete theory of human work if we are to build systems that can support the way people *actually* work, versus treating them as cogs in an information machine.

Now is the time for companies wanting to deploy the Hollywood Model to embrace Human Interaction Management Systems. After fifty years of coping with the limited tools at their disposal, it's time that interaction workers be supported properly by, instead of having to slavishly support, computer systems. High performance teams need capabilities for human interaction management to move beyond the Information Age and into the Process Age.

TAKEAWAY: People don't work in isolation, they work in teams of specialists. Increasingly, those teams are scattered across multiple companies and alliances, across the globe, meaning that optimizing the work of teams, with emerging human interaction management tools is crucial to a company's ability to compete.

7. Extreme Supply Chains

Analyst Deborah Asbrand observed that, "Manufacturers and distributors used to point with pride to their fully stocked, football-field-size warehouses. But no more. High inventory levels are considered evidence of an inefficient supply chain."[32]

Forrester Research proclaimed that, "As trade in every U.S. supply chain moves in some measure to the Internet, Forrester believes that on-line sales will balloon from $43 billion to $1.3 trillion. This change will force businesses to re-tool their relationships, roles, and channels."[33]

What differentiates one company from another in the same market? Several years ago, quality was the key. Then quality and low cost together became the winning combination. But now, quality and cost are givens. *Responsiveness* is now the key to differentiate among competitors. The enterprise that responds to customer needs fastest is the winner. And responsiveness equals cycle time speed. In today's marketplace, production of goods and services requires making products to customer *demand*, not to a *forecast*. This new model requires radical cycle time improvements. The focus shifts to important details of pull-control methods, plus specific methods for designing mixed-model production cells for maximum effectiveness. Answers lie in Kanban pull-type systems, where material is restocked based on usage, not planned consumption.

For years, front-office executives dismissed planning and distribution as hands-dirtying processes that were of minimal importance. "Logistics never got senior management's attention," says Greg Girard, senior analyst in supply-chain management for Advanced Manufacturing Research in Boston.[34] "Distribution was something done at the warehouse and the loading dock."

Not so today with tighter margins and faster cycle-time demands. Supply and demand planning, and end-to-end logistics have become so important that logistics managers have assumed greater status in the organization, often reporting directly to CEOs and COOs.

Procurement of production goods and services (raw materials and resale items) has been the subject of automation for some time. Supply chain management (SCM) systems were implemented in the 1960s by retailers (Wal-Mart is the recognized pioneer in using SCM as a competitive weapon) and have grown to be the norm in manufacturing and distribution industries. As shown in the figure below, SCM spans the full supply chain, from procuring raw materials to delivering finished goods to the ultimate consumers.

Supply Chain Management aims to optimize planning and

execution processes to respond to market demand for goods and services. Processes that are optimized include:

- supply planning
- demand planning
- production planning, and
- inbound/outbound logistics.

The major objectives of supply chain management are getting the right product to the right place, at the right time with the right price. The goals include: reduced cycle time, increased customer satisfaction, reduced inventory and associated costs, reduced product obsolescence, reduced operating expense, reduced working capital, and increased return on assets (ROA).

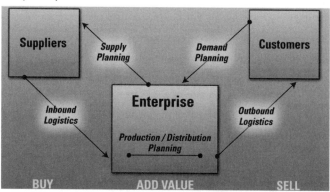

Supply Chain Management

Supply chain goals can be optimized by increasing communication and sharing information across the entire supply chain, from customers and their customers (demand planning) to suppliers and their suppliers (supply planning). Demand and supply planning drive production and distribution planning, which, in turn are determined by inbound and outbound logistics. By sharing information and taking a complete business ecosystem view, all parties can optimize performance and profits.

Grappling with logistics creates a compelling reason for sharing information and operational assets. According to Tim Harmon, international program director in the META Group, supply chains have become a hot issue recently because most forward-thinking companies have completed the automation of their internal operational systems and are now looking outward to their extended systems as areas of potential savings. And these savings are not small. Logistics costs in the United States alone are estimated at $760 billion to $790 billion a year. Worldwide, the annual cost of moving goods is estimated at $2 trillion to $3 trillion. Even a one percent improvement reaps huge savings.[35]

In today's typical SCM environment, suppliers are close trading partners and are tightly integrated via costly and proprietary private "Extranets" as shown in the figure below. Traditional supply chain automation is expensive and complex, thereby excluding small and medium-sized enterprises. Many who do automate do so through coercion. Coercion? Yes, if a big fish in a supply chain, let's say Wal-Mart, tells its suppliers that they must use EDI, they either do EDI or don't do business with Wal-Mart. However, the coercive supply chain model, as the Gartner Group terms it, is about to be history. Analyst Mathew Schwartz explains, "Supply chains used to be exclusive affairs, the playthings of corporate giants who arm-twisted a few of their bigger supply-chain partners into following along."[36]

Although successful implementations of digital techniques certainly have optimized supply chains in many industries, the economics of the Internet have opened up new possibilities for small to medium size enterprises. The Internet provides a platform that allows an enterprise to extend supply chain automation to its suppliers' suppliers and its customers' customers, forming dynamic trading networks: end-to-end *supply webs* containing real-time business process facilities and shared data warehouses of information for decision support.

An *extended* supply chain management system differs with traditional SCM systems in the extent to which a company can integrate with its suppliers, trading partners and customers. Using the Internet platform provides loose and dynamic linkages with multiple suppliers, multiple internal supply chains in multi-line and multi-divisional corporations, and the many small-to-medium enterprise (SME) suppliers that make up to 75% of manufacturing sites.

By sharing information all the way from the point-of-sale to the inventory levels of suppliers' suppliers, all participants in an extended supply chain system can gain competitive advantage. In "The Seven Principles of Supply Chain Management," Anderson, Britt and Farve write, "Rejecting the traditional view of a company and its component parts as distinct functional entities, savvy managers realize that the real measure of success is how well activities coordinate across the supply chain to create value for customers, while increasing the profitability of every link in the chain. In the process, some even redefine the competitive game."[37]

In explaining the successes and failures of SCM initiatives of over 100 manufacturers, distributors and retailers, they conclude of the successes that, "They are typically broad efforts, combining both strategic and tactical change. They also reflect a holistic approach, viewing the supply chain from end to end and orchestrating efforts so that the whole improvement achieved—in revenue, costs, and asset utilization—is greater than the sum of its parts."

"Unsuccessful efforts likewise have a consistent profile. They tend to be functionally defined and narrowly focused, and they lack sustaining infrastructure. Uncoordinated change activity erupts in every department and function and puts the company in grave danger of 'dying the death of a thousand initiatives.' The source of failure is seldom management's difficulty identifying what needs fixing. The issue is determining how to develop and execute a supply chain transformation plan that can move multiple, complex operating entities (both internal and external) in the same direction."

Extreme supply chains are managed end-to-end, not just inside a single company. But there is more. A company must not only manage a single end-to-end supply chain, it must manage multiple supply chains, simultaneously, for different market niches, and often, for individual customers—that's the real challenge of 21st century supply-chain competition.

As Jonathan Byrnes pointed out in "You Only Have One Supply Chain?" "There is a fundamental change occurring in supply chain management. In the past, most companies had relatively static supply chains with a 'one size fits all' orientation. A few had dual supply chains coexisting side by side, but once the configuration was in place, things didn't change much. The static supply chains of the past reflected two factors: (1) Until recently, supply chain IT was not capable of dynamic management; and (2) everyone was in the same boat, so there was little competitive disadvantage. Now things are changing fast. Modern supply chain IT is becoming more capable of dynamic management, assigning the right product to the right supply chain at the right time. Already, some competitors, like Wal-Mart, P&G, and Target, are using these innovations to sprint ahead of the pack."[38]

TAKEAWAY: Companies that used to be tightly linked to

a few suppliers are now finding they must establish and maintain relationships with a *web* of suppliers, often scattered across the globe. They must also manage not one, but multiple supply networks to compete by customizing their offerings for their ever-more-demanding customers.

8. Extreme Experiences & Self-Service

In the *agricultural economy* in Columbia, South American coffee farmers earn about 3 cents a cup for selling their coffee beans as *commodities*.

North of them, a factory in the *industrial economy* of the United States roasts, grinds and packages coffee beans and sells their *goods* for about 25 cents per cup.

Then, in the *service economy*, a restaurant provides a *service* by brewing the coffee and selling it at a dollar a cup—expecting a tip, of course.

Then, in the *experience economy*, along comes Starbucks, which provides an *experience* where that original 3-cent cup of coffee now costs three dollars!

The American economy has evolved from an agricultural to an industrial economy, and then to a service economy. But now it's on to what can best be described as an *experience economy*, where the total experience, not just the goods or services being rendered to the customer, command a premium.

Most people know that planet Earth is the third rock from the Sun, but Starbucks' CEO, Howard Schultz, wants his stores to be "third place" on the third rock from the Sun—a place where people will want to spend their time besides the first place, home, and the second place, work. To achieve that goal, Starbucks must take the 3-cents-a-cup commodity of coffee and transform it into a 3-dollar lifestyle experience. To do that, Starbucks offers its Wi-Fi connections to the Internet, and let's customers create their own music CDs at about a dollar a song. People tend to stay in the shops nine times longer than the usual five minutes of traditional coffee houses, and, of course, they buy more lattés during the stay.

Today's customers don't just want to buy high quality standard products or services—they want to buy high-quality *experiences*, life styles, and they even want the products and services to fulfill their *unarticulated* needs.

We might think of selling experiences in only the domains of the movie house or a trip to Walt Disney World or a stay at the Waldorf. But that's not so.

On Friday nights in Germany, singles looking for romance, or simply flirting, can drop in at their nearest Wal-Mart store where they will get more than everyday low prices. If they wish, they will also be given a big bright red bow to attach to their shopping cart or basket.

The program is called "singles shopping," with Friday being singles night. It's up to the willing participants to approach one another and take it from there. Wal-Mart even has "flirting hot spots" in the stores, stocked with romantic products, such as wine, cheese, chocolates and candles to help break the ice. Wal-Mart is providing everyday, low-priced extreme experiences.

Even the off-putting task of taking your car to a service station for a repair or tune-up can be transformed from an act of drudgery into an experience to look forward to. In a move to ring up higher sales and profits, Jomo, Japan's sixth-largest gas station, remodeled its retail outlets so drivers would actually enjoy waiting for time-consuming services. They wanted to offer fascinating experiences around the boring core offering—car services. Jomo labeled its new venture as *"Value Style,"* and introduced comfortable cafes, kid play areas and massage chairs. Men in blue outfits performed choreographed car washes making the customers applaud. Aftermarket makeover sales soared. Vehicle visits per station went up 22 percent over the previous year, driving a 15 percent sales increase. Jomo has made its *Value Style* service offering a differentiator in an otherwise commodity business. As Jomo creates an upscale atmosphere, it attracts owners of higher-end vehicles who spend more on vehicle maintenance than do economy car owners.

As companies struggle to avoid that dirty word, "commoditization," they can and must consider how they can climb the food chain beyond the planes of offering just goods and services. Returning to the Jomo example for a moment, an auto service company doesn't have to build a playground or dance for its dinner. It could instead provide an experience that would delight the harried car owner—pick up and deliver the customer's car, giving them something they will certainly value, "time."

Although their thesis has been criticized as an example of an over-hyped business philosophy arising from or in the dot-com boom, B. Joseph Pine II and James H. Gilmore, in their book, *The Experience Economy: Work Is Theatre & Every Business a Stage,* offer a strategy for companies to depict and stage the experiences that will greatly increase the economic value of what they offer. They say that to be successful in today's increasingly competitive environment companies must learn to *stage experiences* for each one of their individual customers. A core argument is that because of technology, increasing competition, and the increasing expectations of consumers, services today are starting to look like commodities.

Pine and Gilmore say that "products can be placed on a continuum from undifferentiated commodities to highly differentiated. Just as service markets build on goods markets which in turn build on commodity markets, so transformation and experience markets build on these newly commoditized services, e.g. building on Internet bandwidth to offer sophisticated consulting services. The classification for each stage in the evolution of products is:

- If you charge for undifferentiated stuff, then you are in the commodity business.
- If you charge for distinctive tangible things, then you are in the goods business.
- If you charge for the activities you perform, then you are in the service business.
- If you charge for the feeling customers have because of engaging you, then you are in the experience business.
- If you charge for the benefit customers (or "guests") receive as a result of spending their time, you are in the transformation business."

Now, before trying to leap into some mythical transformational experience business, companies should consider some here-and-now practical strategies that can take them a long way toward better satisfying never-satisfied customers: *process-powered self-service* over the Web.

Web portal pioneer, Pehong Chen, CEO of Broadvision, explains, "To appreciate the benefits of high-touch self-service on the Web, consider the low-touch model that is more prevalent today. When you apply for a loan online, you input your data and wait for the result to come back. The Web is little more than a modem collecting data and displaying results. The application processing occurs in a "black box." You are no longer a participant in the process. You lose visibility into the process. In this scenario, there is no difference between a loan application by Web or by phone.

"In a high-touch self-service model, you retain visibility into the process and remain a participant—receiving alerts and notifications at points in the process that require input, decisions or collaboration with others involved in the process. All participants have visibility into status, action items and previous activity relating to the process. Rule-driven aspects of the process move forward without requiring an intermediary.

"High-touch process-powered self-service harnesses the power of the Web to meet the needs of all participants in the process and to dramatically reduce the cost of providing high quality service and support. Some would argue that it also improves on the quality of service available in the high-touch intermediary model by providing concierge-level service at your desktop. It is an outside-in model that shifts the center of gravity to the people involved in the process—providing customers, partners and employees with processes that respond to their needs rather than requiring them to adapt to your processes."

In short, process-powered self-service is a two-sided coin:

it provides double leverage by cutting costs and increasing customer satisfaction. Web-based self-service "puts customers to work—for free" as employees who handle product configuration, order entry and much after-sale support. This is Dell Computer's well-documented business model, where customers become "prosumers," helping to *produce* that which they *consume*. Process-powered self-service, represents one of the most promising new sources of competitive advantage for the 21st century for companies that learn to deliver it.

TAKEAWAY: People are buying emotions, the feelings that make up the complete experience of consuming a product or service. In the new food chain, companies that continue to provide just products will be commoditized. To compete in the 21st century, companies must provide product services and more: complete experiences that delight their customers, often affecting their lifestyles.

9. Extreme Industry Blur

Competitors in the 20th century were neatly arranged into clearly defined industries, usually contained in geographically-bounded markets. Companies were vertically integrated, owning most facets of production, from raw materials to finished goods. As a company in a given industry, you knew who your competitors were, and you learned to compete against them.

Now, in the 21st century, your competitors are likely to appear from nowhere, below your radar. They scan the globe in a constant search, not just for low-cost labor, but also for innovation. They know no geographic bounds on either their supply chains or their markets. They are laser focused on their branding and their customers, offering more and more products and services to grab an ever greater share of each of their customer's wallets. They don't own the means of production, or often, even the designs of their products, as they plug-in the specialists from around the world into their value-delivery systems. They have their eyes on your customers.

The new playing field is a two-edged sword. While new competitors can enter your industry, you too can become an extreme competitor, aggregating more and more offerings for your customers, and entering markets outside your industry. ExxonMobil is in the gourmet coffee business. Starbucks is in the Internet business. Wal-Mart is in retail banking. eBay is in the telephone business with its acquisition of Skype.

Facing fierce new competition, Cincinnati Bell adopted a "defend and grow" strategy, using bundling to engage in both defensive and offensive plays. In 2004, it launched its "You Add, We Subtract," campaign designed to aggregate total solutions (local, long distance, high-speed Internet and wireless services). The campaign helped add 52,000 customers to its "super bundle." By becoming an early adopter of business process management, the company is positioned with the agility it needs to continue offering more services to its customers as technology continues to blur industry boundaries. Cincinnati Bell is now getting into the digital entertainment business—and who knows what's next? One thing is certain, Cincinnati Bell is no longer just a telephone company.

High-tech gizmos (handycams, laptops and playstations) come to mind when you think of Sony. But the line of business that is producing much of this business superstar's profits is financial services, including insurance. Sony Financial Holdings, formed in April 2004, sells several insurance products: life, accident, medical and auto insurance policies, plus Internet savings accounts. Together these financial services business lines will earn an estimated $509 million in operating profits in 2005, according to estimates from Merrill Lynch & Co. Sony leveraged its customer relationship assets to diversify into financial services. Backed with the idea that Japanese consumers would trust the company that builds their high-tech gizmos to sell them high-quality financial services, and using the slogan, "Love and Trust," Sony quickly jumped over industry walls to disrupt the financial services industry.

In fact, manufacturing is no longer the only business of classic manufacturing companies like Ford and General Motors. Much of their earnings now come from finance-related activities and other services, not from manufacturing activities. GM believed that it could create synergies by selling financial products to customers who bought its cars, so GMAC financial services was created. GMAC has three major businesses. Roughly 55 percent of its business involves auto financing, while the rest revolves around commercial and residential mortgages (Ditech.com). While GM's car business continues to decline due to competition from Toyota, Honda and others, GMAC Financial Services posted net income of $2.9 billion in 2004, marking yet another year of record earnings, and its tenth straight year of increased profits. Similarly, Ford Credit is the financial arm of Ford Motors, which continues to make money while Ford's automobile business is struggling. In fact, even giving away the core product—and making money on services and accessories—has, in fact, become a business strategy, leading to industry lines becoming totally blurred.

Nowhere is industry blur more evident than in the digital world. The relentless evolution of digital technology—faster chips, broadband and software—is making *digital convergence* a driver of industry blur in the consumer electronics industry. We are witnessing a collision of three massive industries namely consumer electronics, software, and communications. The industry walls are coming down, and, in the process, creating new products and services that can't be categorized as computer technology or consumer electronics. Desktop computers, TVs, laptops, personal digital assistants, cell phones (now also cameras), digital music players (iPod, now also a movie player), digital cameras (still or video), video game players (Playstation, Xbox), on demand players (Tivo) . . . the list goes on, are all being networked and are converging to create a single digital ecosystem. Dell and Gateway are selling flat-screen TVs. In August of 2005, Microsoft announced Xbox 360, a video game and entertainment system placed at the center of this digital convergence. Xbox 360 ignites a new era of digital entertainment that is always connected, always personalized, and always in high definition. The home is now the battleground in digital convergence.

This digital convergence is creating huge opportunities for upstarts, and challenges for incumbent companies. Change is now extreme, and companies are still trying to figure out the killer products and services. The dramatic shifts ahead will create ripple effects in other industries like publishing, television programming, and so on. Individual consumers will be able to create their own Internet television shows, movies, radio stations, and online newspapers. It's already happening. Podcasting, the creation of "radio programs" often produced by ordinary people on a variety of topics from politics to food, is on a tear. Podcasts can be downloaded from the Internet into digital music players, giving us a glimpse into the of future of digital entertainment.

The conditions are ripe for upstarts with innovative ideas to create new products and services. TiVo created a personal video recorder allowing users to capture television programming on internal digital storage for later viewing (called "time shifting"). TiVo systems function similarly to VCRs, but use non-removable hard-disk storage, and contain sophisticated software to record programs, not only those the user specifically requests, but also other material the user is likely to be interested in. Consumers can design their own viewing schedules and, to the dismay of advertisers, can bypass advertisements. This has shaken up the advertising industry. TiVo and cable television giant Comcast have teamed up to make TiVo's service available over Comcast's cable network, with the first co-developed products available by the end of 2006, using the TiVo brand.

Digital convergence is pushing companies to venture into unformed markets, far away from their original roots. Fierce competition and constantly changing business plans will become the norm—and translating success from one industry into success into another industry poses immense challenges.

TAKEAWAY: It's not your father's neat and orderly industry any more. Be on guard against competitive threats coming from outside your industry; and get into other industry segments to aggregate more complete solutions for your customers. Listen to Intel's Andy Grove, who tells us that only the paranoid survive.

10. Extreme Education & Learning

In terms of magnitude and speed, we're living in the most

rapidly changing economic period in history—from the agricultural revolution, to the industrial revolution, and now on to the knowledge revolution. Nothing in history compares to what's now hidden in plain sight—the rise of millions of highly educated knowledge workers in low-wage nations.

As newspaper reporter, John Schmid, wrote in 2003, "While the United States focuses on China's export prowess and cheap labor, Beijing is investing in a new generation of sophisticated "knowledge workers" to carry the nation to the next stage of its industrial revolution.

"The nation's 1,300 schools of higher education are critical to China's grand social engineering plan to lift itself up by first becoming the world's manufacturing base, then its knowledge base.

"Already, China has pulled way ahead of the U.S. and the rest of the world by one key measure. China graduates in excess of three times more engineers—electrical, industrial, biochemical, semiconductor, mechanical, even power generation—with bachelor's degrees than the U.S. university system.

"A wave of young software experts, industrial engineers and bio-technology graduates has flowed out of China's fast-growing, industrial-strength university system, and assumed key posts in China's ascendant society. The exponential increase in applied-science graduates mirrors the nation's overall export expansion. Around the time that engineering graduates peaked in the U.S. in 1983, China was just getting going on its 'Four Modernizations,' a movement launched 25 years ago to promote four key sectors of the economy: science and technology; agriculture; industry; and the military."[39]

On April 7, 2005, CnetNews reported, "The University of Illinois tied for 17th place in the world finals of the Association for Computing Machinery International Collegiate Programming Contest. That's the lowest ranking for the top-performing U.S. school in the 29-year history of the competition. Shanghai Jiao Tong University of China took top honors this year, followed by Moscow State University and the St. Petersburg Institute of Fine Mechanics and Optics. Those results continued a gradual ascendance of Asian and East European schools during the past decade or so. A U.S. school hasn't won the world championship since 1997, when students at Harvey Mudd College achieved the honor. 'The U.S. used to dominate these kinds of programming Olympics,' said David Patterson, president of the Association for Computing Machinery and a computer science professor at the University of California, Berkeley."

In 2005, Toyota decided to put a plant to produce RAV4 mini-SUV's in Ontario, Canada. Why did Toyota pass up significant financial incentives for a U.S. site? The reason is simple, the quality of the Canada's work force. The president of the Toronto-based Automotive Parts Manufacturers' Association pointed out that "the educational level in the Southern United States was so low that trainers for Japanese plants in

Alabama had to use 'pictorials' to teach some illiterate workers how to use high-tech equipment."

Paul Krugman noted in his July 25, 2005 column in the *New York Times,* "There's some bitter irony here for Alabama's governor. Just two years ago voters overwhelmingly rejected his plea for an increase in the state's rock-bottom taxes on the affluent, so that he could afford to improve the state's low-quality education system. Opponents of the tax hike convinced voters that it would cost the state jobs."

This comment came five months after earth's richest person, Bill Gates, co-founder of the Bill & Melinda Gates Foundation that gives millions to educational institutions, remarked before the *National Education Summit on High Schools,* "America's high schools are obsolete."

Irony number two concerns chairman Gates, "As chairman of Microsoft, Gates is responsible for a business policy that actively harms public schools. Microsoft maintains a small office in Reno, Nevada—a state with no corporate income tax. Sixty billion dollars in licensing fees for Windows and Office software has passed through that office, and an estimated $300 million in taxes has been lost to the state of Washington for the sale of products produced in Washington. What do we make of this contradiction between Gates the philanthropist and Gates the corporate officer? It is not that Microsoft should become magnanimous—that is the proper (and admirably accomplished) role of the Gates Foundation. But Microsoft, and Gates, should understand that it is not in their best long-term interest to distort the honest relationship that can exist between a community and a corporation. This relationship is not always easy to assess; sometimes there will be honest disagreement about what community and corporation owe each other. But there will be other times when distortion is crystal clear. We can use the duck test: If it walks like a duck and quacks like a duck, it is a duck. The office in Reno walks like a tax evasion; it quacks like a tax evasion; it is a tax evasion. Microsoft's familiar advertising slogan, 'Your potential, our passion' is undercut by every transaction made in that Reno office. With every transaction, and with every unpaid tax dollar, Microsoft's (business) passion reduces children's potential, by making it harder to adequately fund our schools," Paul Shannon noted in the *Seattle-Post Intelligencer*.

Now, whether you love or hate either Krugman or Gates is not the point here. Instead, the point is that, as a business person, you know the need for a highly skilled workforce, and you know that education is key to creating such a workforce.

An August 2005 report, *Getting Smarter, Becoming Fairer,* included statistics that, "the United States ranked 24th out of 29 nations in math literacy. Only 1.6% of 24-year-olds in the United States have a bachelor's degree in engineering, compared to figures roughly two times higher in Russia, three times higher in China, and four times higher in South Korea and Japan. The number of American engineering graduates peaked in 1985 and is presently down 20% from that level; the percentage of United States undergraduates taking engineering is the second lowest of all developed countries. China, India, and other nations compete more effectively to develop their own human capital and economic advantage.

"America has more than simply jobs at stake. In the United States, a vibrant democracy and a powerful economy are inextricably linked. Our economy has buoyed our democratic traditions, and these traditions have in turn bolstered our economy. Today, this powerful and productive interplay is at risk, and our security, about which we are so rightly concerned, is threatened along with it. Our outmoded system of education is steadily eroding those strengths, with the same effect over time as a military defeat: narrow life choices, constricted economic conditions and a growing cynicism that infects and poisons civic life. The effect may seem slow and incremental at first, but the long-term impact will not be. It will be all the more painful and inexcusable because we have had full warning of the threat and its consequences. Almost a quarter of a century has passed since the National Commission on Excellence in Education told us that continuing neglect of our educational system was akin to 'committing an act of unthinking, unilateral educational disarmament.' We like to think that we have engaged in serious educational reform since then. But, to date, we have made mostly cosmetic changes and tinkered at the margins."

It's now common knowledge that the American education system is broken. Many also know that funding for research has been slashed. The current administration cut the National Science Foundation budget by $100 million in 2005, and in 2006 has proposed shrinking the Department of Energy science programs and basic and applied research in the Department of Defense.

So the point is that you cannot count on government to solve the education problem and other infrastructure problems, including basic research; even though education, a skilled work force, research and infrastructure form the pillars of a competitive society.

So it's up to *you* to take on America's learning deficit. It's time for some out-of-the-box thinking, like education process insourcing (EPI). Instead of outsourcing jobs to India, insourcing means working in the U.S. virtually, via the Net. Capitalizing on the shortage of teachers in the U.S., especially in subjects like mathematics, Indian tutors are finding online education a good revenue spinner in this emerging segment in outsourcing. An offshoot of business process outsourcing (BPO), EPI is India's new emerging service offering, and it's getting wide support from both students and clients in the U.S., Singapore and other countries.

According to some estimates, 40 percent of the students in America fail in mathematics, and the country needs close to one million new teachers over the next ten years. "While the US faces a severe shortage of quality mathematics teachers, in India we have surplus skilled manpower," said Santanu Prakash, CEO of Educomp, an Indian company that brings live tutors to the U.S. without the tutors leaving their seats in India. Educomp is targeting one million students by 2010.

According to an India Times report, "Sitting in small cubicles, fitted with a headset and pen mouse, these tutors are teaching students subjects like mathematics (and even English!) from course curriculums specified in the U.S.—in an accent familiar to Americans. The service is given through a software called 'White Board' in both voice and text platforms. The student and teacher can see each other over the computer and talk on the head phone."[40]

Currently, private tutoring is an $8 billion industry in the U.S. and growing at 12 percent a year. Of that, $3 billion is accounted for by tutoring through the Internet. By the end of 2005, an estimated 77 million students under the age of 18 will have Internet access, and thus to the e-tutoring format.

Then there is Heymath.com. This small firm in Chennai, India, provides mathematics homework help to students over the Internet, and, please note, lesson plans to teachers. Its initial target market was the Singapore public education system, but after successfully selling its product there, it is now expanding elsewhere. For those initially concerned about quality, Cambridge University in England is also part of the equation, providing the overall quality controls and certifying the lesson plans and teaching methods. HeyMath! is recommended by Cambridge's Millennium Mathematics Project, and endorsed by the Singapore Teachers' Union. Raghuram Rajan, the Director of Research for the International Monetary Fund, sits on the board. The teachers, from the Indian Institute of Technology in Chennai, not only go online to tutor students in Singapore (from grade six to twelve) on their math homework, they also help teachers in Singapore develop lesson plans and prepare PowerPoint presentations or jazzy ways to teach math. All this is paid for by the public school system in Singapore.

These nascent tutoring and other education insourcing services provide but a glimpse of the new possibilities for taking on America's education crisis, even without reforming our own school systems, even without leadership from our governments, even without the tough political battles it would take to reinvent and refund American educational institutions. As a business leader and as a parent, you now have a direct path of action. As in-home schooling continues to grow, complete curriculums can be delivered with education insourcing. Some insourced tutoring offerings are being delivered by public libraries, opening this game-changing resource to even the poorest students who want to learn.

If we extend the HeyMath!-Singapore initiative to the notion of an Education Management Organization (EMO), we could go well past private tutoring offerings and, perhaps, in the form of charter schools, enter into the public education arena. Combine the Net-ready $100 laptop PC that M.I.T. wants to manufacture (with the help of Google, Advanced

Micro Devices, News Corp., Red Hat and BrightStar) with WiMax (wireless broadband) Internet access; and the public education system, designed 100 years ago, could be dragged kicking and screaming into the 21st century—at a fraction of today's costs.

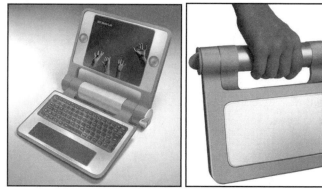

M.I.T.'s Design for a $100, Net-ready Laptop PC

Student hours at expensive red-brick school houses could be cut in half, doubling the capacity for the existing physical plant which is now under great stress. Under the shortened hours model, students would go to the school house primarily to learn social interaction skills and participate in physical education. Then they go home to their live teachers on the Net to learn the rest, taking on math, science, reading and writing *at their own pace,* with one-on-one and small-group interactions, along with powerful interactive learning tools embodied with infinite patience. Virtual classes for totally accredited courses could be formed with students and teachers anywhere. Grouping learners at the same achievement levels, and pairing them with master teachers in Bangalore, Pretoria or Peoria could easily be facilitated. Students could Skype each other, tutor each other, work together on team problems, and form friendships and social bonds.

Companies not happy with the knowledge levels of their employees can start offering these cyberspace resources to their employees instead of the usual land-based tuition reimbursement offerings at local classroom-based institutions. Specialized skills training is another obvious use for education insourcing and the globalization of education. A million highly qualified teachers, technology trainers and curriculum builders are now at your fingertips.

With super-specialized skills being the price of admission to tomorrow's jobs, and with the broken education system in America, one M.I.T. researcher, who wants to remain anonymous, is dreaming up a way for individuals to empower themselves, over and over again through lifelong learning. He's addressing the problem encapsulated when the CEO of the outsourcing firm, NeoIT, Atul Vashistha, told the *LA Times,* "If you're a Web programmer, I'm sorry, you have no right to think you can keep your job in the U.S. if you're using the same technology that existed four years ago. You've got to keep moving up. You've got to keep going back to school. If you're not going to do that, you're going to lose your job."

The problem with this scenario is that going back to school means going back to expensive, broken, and out-of-date schools if you are a Web programmer with 4-year old HTML skills. The M.I.T. researcher's vision is "Teachers Sans Borders." He wants to be the meteor that hits the earth and wipes out the dinosaurs of education. That would have been a pipe dream just a few years ago. But by deploying technologies from Skype, the free Internet telephone and video conferencing service, why not sign up for low cost, highly specialized courses delivered straight to your computer at home to upgrade your XML and Web services skills.

Hmm, a traditional satellite up/downlink in the U.S. to

reach a professional trainer in India with leading-edge Web programming knowledge is $8,000. Skype video is $0.00.

Fully educated, trained and certified English teachers in India are pleased with a monthly salary of 10,000 rupees ($230), twice what they would earn in entry-level jobs at local schools. When you do the math, the solution to America's education problem becomes obvious to even the most casual observer.

If Indians have been coming to America for years to get the best possible education, but are now better educated than Americans, why shouldn't Americans go to school in India—without leaving home?

An August 2005 article by Thomas Peeler appeared in the *Sarasota Herald Tribune* that sums up the challenge of extreme education, "During the next several months, taxpayers will be challenged to vote for or against the Sarasota County School District's proposed 1-mill tax rate. I understand the reasoning behind either course of action. However, there is an educational crisis looming in the global economy.

"American education is in a crisis, and the next few years will determine how our country will react to the crisis. Most people are worried about outsourcing high-tech jobs to countries like India and China. Why? Dalian, a port city in China, has 22 universities and colleges with 200,000 students. More than half of those students graduate with engineering degrees, and the students who are studying history or literature are directed to study English, Japanese and computer science, so they will be employable. Remember, this is just one city in China.

"India is no different. Hundreds of thousands of Indians compete to get into the prestigious Indian Institute of Technology. Companies such as IBM, Microsoft, HP, Texas Instruments and 3M have offices in Bangalore, India (India's Silicon Valley)."

Peeler goes on to write that there are, "many other examples of countries that have entered the *brain race*. Businesses around the world no longer follow the money; they are following the brains. The educational developments in countries like China and India are new; we have yet to feel the full impact of thousands of highly trained engineers and scientists hitting the global employment market.

"The Sarasota district has many very good schools and ranks among the best districts in Florida. However, in today's global economy, that is not enough. The district must become world class. NeXt Generation Learning will help ensure that. Our students will be prepared to compete against the world's best and brightest."

Such debates are good. But reforming and funding the massive federal bureaucracy in the U.S. (already hell bent on cutting funds for infrastructure, social services, research and education) will be like turning a neo-conservative aircraft carrier on a dime. With Skype or Google Talk on the other hand, watch for Teachers Sans Borders to come to a PC near you, delivering excellence in basic education, training and life-long learning.

TAKEAWAY: Up-to-date skills are essential for maintaining a competitive edge. A skilled and knowledgeable workforce is vital to any company, but American education is increasingly obsolete and failing. Smart companies increasingly will turn to global alternatives in education and skills training—for their children and their employees. Today's options were not possible prior to the advent of broadband Internet connections and the rise of a pool of world-class, credentialed educators, in countries such as India. But now we have new options to provide life-long, personalized education and training that's tailored to the individual learner. Distance is now removed from the learning equation.

11. Extreme Government

The 21st century *mandate* for business is Do More With Less. The 21st century *imperative* for business is Business Process Management (BPM)—a technology-enabled transformation of how work gets done, how business is accomplished. The 21st century *mandate* for government is Do More With Less. The 21st century *imperative* for government is Business Process Management. The Aberdeen Group summarizes, "Business Process Management enables government agencies to dismantle obsolete bureaucratic divisions by cutting the labor- and paper-intensive inefficiency from manual, back-end processes. Faster and auditable processes allow employees to do more in less time, reducing paper use as well as administrative overhead and resources. The BPM category may arguably provide the greatest return on investment compared to any other category available on the market today."

In the great 21st century transformation, governments around the world have one major focus: tearing down silos of information maintained by separate agencies that currently stand between their citizens and more efficient public services. As the private sector pushes to provide more convenient 24x7 services, citizens, now known as "customers," will no longer tolerate insulated, disconnected government agencies. Collaboration is becoming the imperative as citizens and businesses demand services independent of agency boundaries. And they don't care to understand how various departments might be involved behind the scenes in delivering those services.

"Most people are talking about the concept of seamless government, a one-stop shop," says Australian Executive Director, Smart Service Queensland, Jane King. "Some have taken a sort of one-inch wide, 10-mile deep view and tried to do a full end-to-end process. Others have gone across the board and said: 'Okay, let's just try and get them all together in a one-stop shop.'"

The isolated islands of information that continue to plague government agencies also pose one of the bigger threats to national security. So in the post-September 11 world, the U.S. government, in particular, is determined to tear down the walls between security agencies and between agencies responsible for customs and border protection to create "one face at the border."

Realizing the new nirvana of joined-up government is a high-wire balancing act. Governments must not only grapple with most of the same complex issues preoccupying the private sector, they also face the added pressures that come with having to consider a myriad of tangled issues around accountability, privacy, politics and policy. Tearing down silos of information requires the organizing of Web portals around customer groups and topics, rather than agency names. Examples of cross-agency portals include: students, people with disabilities and exporters. But instead of just serving up zillions of documents, portals must allow their users to actually "do business" online.

It's two sides of the same coin: users should be able to select an appropriate gateway—citizens, businesses, nonprofits, and federal employees—to find exactly what they need. Then, from their computers, the users should, under policy-governed controls and mechanisms, apply for student financial assistance, buy government publications, apply for social security benefits, request an export license, apply for a passport, and so on. It's the combination of the "finding" and the "doing" that will make government effective, and that's why process-powered e-government is imperative.

So the Australian Taxation Office (ATO) is implementing the ATO Change Program, which is beginning to provide easier, cheaper and more personalized interactions, information and advice for individuals, businesses and tax agents. As outlined by the Commissioner of Taxation, Michael Carmody, the Program is not about tax policies or laws, but about the *experience* that clients have in the tax system. One of the ways in which the ATO will do this is by allowing "customers" to "do business" with them online.

A successful integration of the ATOs systems with those of other government departments (such as welfare provider Centrelink and the Health Insurance Commission) is allowing citizens to access more and more public services online, while helping the government gain a better understanding of the needs of individual citizens and offer a more personalized service to suit those needs.

Just how formidable such tasks are was suggested in August, 2005, when Australian *Computerworld* revealed the Australian Government's e-Health initiatives had medical companies fuming over time-consuming software, and parents traumatized over automatic rebates that not only don't arrive, but also disrupted childcare arrangements. It also described how parents applying for automatic rebates from Medicare-funded childhood immunizations were out of pocket and chasing paper (after Centrelink was forced to manually process payments for about 635,000 childhood immunization payments) because verification data meant to be submitted online by doctors wasn't turning up in the IT systems of the

Health Insurance Commission (HIC).

Even so, with an ever increasing number of compensation cases on the books each year, the HIC is streamlining the many administrative tasks involved in managing each case, while avoiding double payments to claimants. The system for the statutory authority is currently handling more than 100,000 compensation cases per annum as well as inward and outward correspondence for more than 400 cases daily—many of these with a lifecycle of between three to five years.

In the U.K., Capgemini is three years into a ten-year Public-Private Partnering arrangement with the Ministry of Defense (MoD) for the provision and management of a secure eCommerce hub for the efficient processing of all supplier interactions with the MoD—known as the Defense eCommerce System. Thousands of suppliers are now using the hub, and the MoD has plans to add additional applications to this robust and secure environment to enable further services.

Also in the U.K. the Harlow District Council, located in the heart of the Essex and Hertfordshire countryside and providing more than 35 different services to a population of 80,000, has consolidated the different channels of communication into a single contact center operation providing customers with a focal point of contact and providing a professional level of service. A fully integrated system, linking data from all departments and services, is breaking down information silos across departments. Since the Council implemented a process-driven system where business can actually get done, citizen satisfaction levels have more than doubled to an all-time high of 94 percent, first-point-of-contact resolution rates have risen by 30 percent, and back-line service responsiveness has increased from 39 percent to 88 percent.

The U.S. Treasury Community Development Financial Institutions (CDFI) Fund, created to expand the availability of credit, investment capital, and financial services for distressed urban and rural communities, was once drowning under a weight of paper. Now a process-driven Web portal is allowing electronic applications to interact with all back-office processing performed via automated workflow. Institutions apply for funding online, and all applicant data is securely stored in the Fund's database, where it is available for internal use. The system is tracking more than one thousand CDFI Fund grants, loans, tax credits, and disbursement and certification applications a year while providing instant access to critical applicant and grant information. Furthermore, because the technology solutions feature an open architecture, it is vastly simplifying the chore of tying together multiple systems and has facilitated communication with other federal government agencies. For example, FCBS has integrated the eGrants process with the Bureau of Public Debt (BPD), which is the federal agency that actually disperses the funds. The cost savings let it better work within its budget.

And new technologies are helping governments with fraud control, too. Louisiana's Fraud and Recovery Section of the Department of Social Services Office of Family Support (OFS) is using new-generation technology to manage its investigative processes and enhance efficiency. Workflow lets each investigator investigate more cases and monitor caseload weaknesses to determine cases that are being worked inefficiently. Integrating workflow with a geographic information system (GIS) lets existing fraud case data be associated with the physical locations of fraudulent activity; thus providing intelligence on the patterns of fraud within geographic areas so fraud can be detected and prosecuted sooner.

And when changes to the province of British Columbia's

Securities Act demanded modifications to the British Columbia Securities Commission's (BCSC) approach to business
processes, workflow technology provided the solution. The
BCSC is an independent government agency responsible for
regulating trading in securities in the province, overseeing
several regulatory processes such as monitoring financial dis-
closure documents and applications for initial public offerings. The high-tech initiative allows active and historical
processes to be shared online with staff across the BCSC's
divisions in real time. Work can be routed automatically during the prospectus review process, meaning fewer errors from
re-keying data and manually tracking paper-based files.

Next generation, process-oriented technology can be a
lifesaver for those on the frontlines of service delivery. For
instance, when the mission depends on the goodwill of thousands of volunteer firefighters, being able to communicate
effectively with them is more than a business challenge: it's a
matter of life and death. In Australia the state of Victoria's
Country Fire Authority (CFA) is forging ahead with a strategy, which embraces eight key projects and is supported by a
"future systems framework" designed to ensure agreement at
fairly high levels about the CFA's information management
objectives. To be implemented over four years, the framework—which has already seen implementation of a finance
system via a resource-sharing arrangement with the CFA's
metropolitan firefighting cousins—is proving a powerful
means of ensuring alignment. The most critical of the eight
projects is the emergency management system, which provides the mission-critical management of the people and
equipment at and around the fire ground, and a supporting
locality information system. This contains all the information
the authority has about a particular location, including satellite

imagery, information about local risks such as the existence of dangerous goods in industrial areas, educational activities the authority has undertaken in the area, operational pre-plans and more.

Government agencies that want to increase their effectiveness in this new way of operating must bite the bullet and take on the challenge of making process, *not* the serving up of raw data, the basic unit of computer-based automation and support. They must shift their focus from "systems of data" to "systems of action-oriented processes." In short, "data processing" must give way to "process processing" if agencies are to actually deliver services and not just data and documents. This concept extends beyond publicly accessible portals and on to the back office of government operations.

Take the way the Australian Department of Finance & Administration faced the major challenge of processing, tracking and dealing with the large volume of information related to ministerial operations (including the Ministerial Briefing, Question Time briefing, Parliamentary questions and cabinet meetings), as well as all ministerial correspondence. To address these challenges the Department created the Parliamentary Workflow System (PaWS) to promote better staff collaboration with process consistency. The high-tech solution has helped the Department to make processes run more efficiently, and gives it the agility it needs to respond to changing conditions, new regulations, and higher demands for service.

For governments, the challenge is not only to do more with less resources and effort, but rather to do more by working smarter. In the 21st century, "citizens" are now being treated more like "customers" than minions. Those government customers will accept nothing less than the level of service provided by the private sector where companies must compete to gain their loyalty.

There is, however, more to extreme government besides working smarter. Governments now have no choice but to foster economic competitiveness for their nations if they are to thrive among the three billion new capitalists that China, India and the former Soviet Union have brought to the party.

Even small steps can count in fostering innovation and removing bureaucratic friction. Time was when the least required of a farmer was to be, well, "down on the farm." Now there's a phrase which doesn't have the same resonance it once did, with down-under Australian farmers about to get the ability to open their farm gates remotely from anywhere in the world via a signal sent over the Internet. They'll even be able to watch online as their gates open and let cattle through, thanks to a government-led initiative by The University of New England (UNE) and part-government owned telco, Telstra. This initiative lets them use mobile phones for security surveillance and stock monitoring, and receive text messages every time a gate is opened. Meanwhile, on their farm or off, Welsh farmers dependant on subsidies granted through the European Union's Common Agricultural Policy (CAP) program are getting those subsidies substantially faster thanks to automated claims processing. Delays in processing farmer's subsidy claims can not only hit their businesses but the local economy as well. So the National Assembly for Wales has provided a solution that clears claims in hours, allows program administrators to maintain the system directly, and makes it far easier to process the multitude of new rules and regulations coming out of Brussels each year.

Some governments are betting the farm to ensure competitive effectiveness of their nations. In August 2005, this author met with Hitoshi Shirai, Deputy General Manager of the Hitachi Research Institute, at a resort on the shores of Tampa Bay. Shirai had traveled from Tokyo on a mission.

In January 2001, the Government of Japan set forth an ambitious goal of making Japan the "World's Most Advanced IT Nation in 2005." An IT Strategic Headquarters unit was established within the Cabinet Office of the Prime Minister of Japan. As Japan glances backwards today to review the implementation of its previously stated goals, it is simultaneously engaged in a forward-leaning decision process of framing a new national IT strategy. President of Hitachi, Etsuhiko Shoyama has been tasked by Prime Minister Koizumi to conduct a review of past performance. As the Chief Researcher at the prestigious Hitachi Research Institute (HRI), Shirai-san, in equal measure, has set his horizons ahead and aims to frame a vision strategy of a future IT-ubiquitous society, extending into 2010 and beyond.

Mr. Shirai and this author discussed three particular themes in some depth. First, we discussed the extent to which "infrastructural technologies" have ceased to become tools of corporate competitive advantage—given availability increases, cost decreases and the narrow time-window of reaping the benefits of such innovations prior to their inevitable commoditization. In what respect does this impact the production of innovation in IT, and productivity in the larger economy? Second, we explored the question, if an IT-ubiquitous society is truly one where computers exist everywhere and can be hooked up with any kind of machine, how far are we from realizing such an environment? And third, and most importantly, we talked about what to do with all of this "raw" interconnectivity. The third topic led to the most in-depth discussion, one centered on the human interaction systems that would be needed to bring all this connectivity to life for a higher purpose than just connectivity: improving how people work, how they learn, how they conduct business, and how they can contribute to society.

Japan fully understands the rise of China and the new realities of globalization and Internet technologies. After all, it was Japan that taught the world economics lessons in the 1980s, and they have never been satisfied with those successes of yesterday. Japan is all about continuous improvement, and its government is spending its political capital to ensure its national economic competitiveness in the new world of extreme competition. In short, the Japanese government "gets it." Does the current American administration?

To find out, let's repeat a quote from earlier in this book where Clyde Prestowitz wrote in the *San Francisco Chronicle*, "According to our elite economists, America's future lies with high tech—with companies like Intel and IBM. Yet here are two of U.S. high-tech industry's top CEOs saying their future may lie abroad, especially in China. Add the fact that U.S.

trade in high-tech products has swung from a surplus to a deficit, and it is not at all clear that this country's future will be in high tech. At the heart of the problem is the false assumption that all the countries in the globalization contest are playing the same game. They're not. Some countries have strategies, but others don't have a clue. The United States is in the latter category."

Corporations and nations have become decoupled. An important part of corporate strategy among the global players is that they simultaneously have more or less given up any loyalty toward any particular nation's interest (since their only motivation is delivering shareholder value), and have increasingly included manipulation of government policy in their corporate strategies.

Prestowitz also wrote, "We desperately need to reinvent globalization. For starters, Washington might become as interested in keeping Intel and IBM building factories at home as Beijing is eager to lay down the red carpet for them."[41]

So, what is the current American administration doing about all this? Before jumping straight to the answer, reflect on the fact that it wasn't dot-com entrepreneurs in Silicon Valley that invented the Internet, it was a government agency called DARPA (the Defense Advanced Research Projects Agency). DARPA was established in response to a major competitive threat the surfaced in 1957, the Soviet launching of Sputnik. Established in 1958, DARPA's mission was to keep U.S. technology ahead of its enemies. DARPA has around 240 personnel (about 140 technical) directly managing a $2 billion budget. These figures are "on average" since DARPA focuses on short-term (two to four-year) projects run by small, purpose-built teams. ARPA was its original name, then it was renamed DARPA (for Defense) in 1972,

then back to ARPA in 1993, and then back to DARPA again
in 1996. It was ARPA that was responsible for funding development of ARPANET (which grew into the Internet), as
well as the Berkeley version of Unix. Now consider what the
current American administration is doing: cutting DARPA's
basic research budget!

In "Pulling the plug on science?" Peter Spotts, staff writer
of *The Christian Science Monitor,* wrote, "From Voyager space-
craft to atom smashers, America's long-term research faces an
era of budget cuts. For decades, American scientists have
unlocked nature's secrets, generated an enormous number of
patents, and earned a string of Nobel Prizes. These days,
however, pride of accomplishment is mingling with angst as
Washington contemplates research cuts on everything from
space weather to high-energy physics. The concern? The
United States unwittingly may be positioning itself for a long,
steady decline in basic research—a key engine for economic
growth—at a time when competitors from Europe and Asia
are hot on America's heels."

While the American administration is heads down on terrorism, other countries are heads up on education, research
and innovation. In November 2004, President George W.
Bush, and China's President Hu Jintao, an engineer, traveled
through Asia. Fareed Zakaria was in the region a few weeks
afterward and was struck by how almost everyone he spoke
with rated Jintao's visits as far more successful than Bush's.
Karim Raslan, a Malaysian writer, explained: "Bush talked
obsessively about terror. He sees all of us through that one
prism. Yes, we worry about terror, but frankly that's not the
sum of our lives. We have many other problems. We're re-
tooling our economies, we're wondering how to deal with the
rise of China, we're trying to address health, social and envi-

ronmental problems. Hu talked about all this; he talked about our agenda, not just his agenda." From Indonesia to Brazil, China is winning new friends.

"The U.S. is like a frog that is slowly boiling in water. It doesn't jump out because it doesn't notice it is about to die."[42] So says Nobel laureate, Steven Chu, director of the Lawrence Berkeley National Laboratory in California, about growing concerns that complacency will lead to the U.S. losing its global scientific pre-eminence within a decade. Chu is a member of the National Academies of Sciences committee that published the October 2005 report, *Rising Above the Gathering Storm*. One significant stumbling block, says the report, is immigration policy. "After 9/11 we became less welcoming," says Chu, who helped draft the recommendations. "We must more than reverse that now." Meanwhile, China and India are investing heavily in their university systems. China produces eight times as many graduate engineers as the U.S., and India five times as many. And U.S. students are falling behind: 12th-graders recently performed below the international average for 21 countries on a test of general mathematics and science knowledge. The NAS report advises the U.S. government to boost investment in education and research by $5 to $7 billion per year, not a lot of money, compared with the roughly $8 billion a *month* spent on Afghanistan and Iraq.

Indeed, governments have leadership roles in supporting 21st century competitive advantage for their nations. Americans could remain unaware of the current realities, and wake up to Prestowitz's "great shift of wealth and power to the East." Now is the time for business leaders to ask their political leaders what their country can do for them in science, research and education.

TAKEAWAY: The governments of Korea, India, Japan

and China have made major strides in giving their countries a competitive edge through investing in infrastructure, science, research and education. They have a strategy for 21st century competition, while as Clyde Prestowitz points out, Washington does not. It's now time for business leaders to demand more from government to refresh initiatives in science, research and education.

12. Extreme Health Care.

Ever wonder who would be the Bill Gates of health care? We'll get to that in a moment, but first let's consider the state of health care in America, and the deep problems this state has created for businesses, large and small.

Tired of waiting for politicians to fix the health care mess in America? Your company can no longer pay for the extreme cost of providing health care to your employees? General Motors, in dancing with Chapter 11 bankruptcy in 2005, estimated that over $1,500 of the cost of a car today is composed of health care costs for its present and retired employees. What are your political leaders doing to take on this dire situation? In short, nothing.

Even worse, with the aging of Americans, many currently in power are looking to cut the flagship social health programs. As with education, we'll just have to look elsewhere, not to our political leaders, for changing the game in health care if our companies are to have any social objectives beyond being raw profit making machines. Again, as with education, we can turn to globalization, and here's how.

Think about a scenario where companies provide health savings accounts for routine medical needs: a broken arm, a bout with the flu or a physical exam. But when it comes to major health requirements such as hip replacement or bypass surgery or long-term care, or major procedures your health insurance company now disallows, your employees and retirees take a quick flight to Cancun or Tijuana or The Bahamas, where they'll receive personal world-class, treatment and care. While there, they'll also avoid the outrageous prescription drug costs by tapping offshore supply chains operated by their health care providers.

Well there isn't such a company in the Western hemisphere—yet. But this man, Dr. Prathap C. Reddy, just could make that happen. He just could become the Bill Gates of health care.

Two decades ago, Dr. Reddy lost a patient who couldn't make it from India to Texas for an open heart surgery. This was the milestone in the Indian Healthcare Industry. Today people have the opportunity in India to receive the best that healthcare has to offer worldwide. Driven by a deep urge to create a world-class medical infrastructure in India and make it more accessible and affordable to a large cross section of India's people, Dr. Reddy opted to give up his successful practice in the U.S. to return to India in the early eighties. Thus, Dr. Reddy began what was truly the process of revolutionizing the path of the Indian Healthcare Industry.

But that's not all. Reddy's Apollo Hospital Group attracted investment from units of Schroders PLC in the U.K., and Citigroup Inc. and Goldman Sachs Group Inc. in the U.S. Sharp drops in Indian tariffs, meanwhile, allowed the company to import gear almost as soon as it appeared in Western hospitals. With barriers down, Dr. Reddy expanded rapidly. He formed a joint venture with the state government in New Delhi to build and finance a new hospital and franchised Apollo's services to bring 45 new clinics to other parts of India.

Having steered the Apollo Hospital Group to a number of locations within India, Dr. Reddy embarked on an Asian expansion plan with the first clinic in Dubai, established in March 1999. He also signed deals with hospitals in Kuwait, Sri Lanka and Nigeria to contract out the company's management services. Today, Apollo operates in eight countries across South Asia, the Middle East and Africa.

Great ideas, of course require validation. What has Apollo accomplished so far?

- Patients: 7.4 million
- Total Number of Employees: over 10,000
- Total Number of Surgeries: 280,000 major, 500,000 minor
- Heart Surgeries: 48,000 - success rate of 98.5%
- Neuro Surgeries: 10,538
- Total Number of Renal Transplants: over 5,000
- Total Number of Master Health Check-ups: 15,000
- Total Number of Beds: 6,400
- Total Number of Hospitals: 45

Yet, those are cold statistics. Let's turn to *Washington Post* Foreign Service reporter, John Lancaster, who tells the story of Howard Staab, a small business owner. "Three months ago, Howard Staab learned that he suffered from a life-threatening heart condition and would have to undergo surgery at a cost of up to $200,000—an impossible sum for the 53-year-old carpenter from Durham, N.C., who has no health insurance. So he outsourced the job to India.

"Taking his cue from cost-cutting U.S. businesses, Staab flew about 7,500 miles to the Indian capital, where doctors at the Escorts Heart Institute & Research Centre—a sleek aluminum-colored building across the street from a bicycle-rickshaw stand—replaced his balky heart valve with one harvested from a pig. Total bill: about $10,000, including round-trip airfare and a planned side trip to the Taj Mahal.

"The Indian doctors, they did such a fine job here, and took care of us so well," said Staab, a gentle, pony tailed bicycling enthusiast who was accompanied to India by his partner, Maggi Grace. "I would do it again."

"Staab is one of a growing number of people who are traveling to India in search of First World health care at Third World prices. Last year, an estimated 150,000 foreigners visited India for medical procedures, and the number is increas-

ing at the rate of about 15 percent a year, according to Za-
kariah Ahmed, a health care specialist at the Confederation of
Indian Industries. Before they would admit him for surgery,
Staab, the heart patient, said hospital officials at Durham Regional Hospital asked for a $50,000 deposit and warned that
the entire cost of treatment could run as high as $200,000."

"Eager to cash in on the trend, posh private hospitals are
beginning to offer services tailored for foreign patients, such
as airport pickups, Internet-equipped private rooms and
package deals that combine, for example, tummy-tuck surgery
with several nights in a maharajah's palace. Some hospitals are
pushing treatment regimens that augment standard medicine
with yoga and other forms of traditional Indian healing.

"The phenomenon is another example of how India is
profiting from globalization—the growing integration of
world economies—just as it has already done in such other
service industries as insurance and banking, which are outsourcing an ever-widening assortment of office tasks to the
country. The trend is still in its early stages. On the other
hand, India offers a growing number of private 'centers of
excellence' where the quality of care is as good or better than
that of big-city hospitals in the United States or Europe, asserted Naresh Trehan, a self-assured cardiovascular surgeon
who runs Escorts and performed the operation on Staab.
Trehan said, for example, that the death rate for coronary bypass patients at Escorts is 0.8 percent. By contrast, the 1999
death rate for the same procedure at New York-Presbyterian
Hospital, where former president Bill Clinton recently un-
derwent bypass surgery, was 2.35 percent, according to a
2002 study by the New York State Health Department.

"Escorts is one of only a handful of treatment facilities
worldwide that specialize in robotic surgery, which is less in-

vasive than conventional surgery because it relies on tiny, re-
mote-controlled instruments that are inserted through a small
incision. Our surgeons are much better," boasted Trehan, 58,
a former assistant professor at New York University Medical
School, who said he earned nearly $2 million a year from his
Manhattan practice before returning to India to found Escorts in 1988.

"Although they are equipped with state-of-the-art technology, hospitals such as Escorts typically are able to charge
far less than their U.S. and European counterparts because
pay scales are much lower and patient volumes higher, according to Trehan and other doctors. For example, a mag-
netic resonance imaging (MRI) scan costs $60 at Escorts,
compared with roughly $700 in New York, according to Tre-
han. Moreover, a New York heart surgeon has to pay
$100,000 a year in malpractice insurance. Here it's $4,000.

"Tom Raudaschl, an Austrian who lives in Canada and
earns his living as a mountain guide suffered from os-
teoarthritis in his hip. Raudaschl last year decided to undergo
'hip resurfacing,' a relatively new procedure that involves
scraping away damaged bone and replacing it with chrome
alloy. 'As soon as you tell people that you're going to India,
they frown,' Raudaschl said. But he said he could not be more
pleased with the service. 'They picked me up at the airport,
did all the hotel bookings, and the food is great, too,' said
Raudaschl, whose private room was equipped with Internet
service, a microwave and a refrigerator. Most important, Raudaschl said the surgeon told him he would be 'skiing again in
a month.'

"To cope with its backlog of cases, Britain's National
Health Service has begun referring patients for treatment to
Spain and France, although for now, the health service limits

referrals to hospitals within three hours' flying time, according to Anupam Sibal, a British-trained pediatrician and Apollo's director of medical services."

That's where The Bahamas, Cancun and Tiajuana come in—as the Apollo model becomes transplanted in those locations. American businesses could provide world-class health care at third world prices within three hours of flight time.

Again the question, what about quality? Let's return to Tom Raudaschl. "Raudaschl flew from Calgary to Chennai, on India's east coast, where a surgeon at Apollo Hospital performed the operation for $5,000, including all hospital costs. Nobody even questions the capability of an Indian doctor, because there isn't a big hospital in the United States where there isn't an Indian doctor working."

Apollo's range of medical services is wide and deep, from the back office to the operating room. The company has capitalized on the high cost of health care administration in the U.S. Hundreds of Apollo's data processors work late-night shifts providing billing services and processing insurance claims for U.S. hospitals and insurers. Apollo laboratories perform clinical trials for Western drug companies, such as Pfizer Inc. and Eli Lilly & Co. Apollo even remotely evaluates X-rays and CAT scans.

The globalization of health care is not limited to Apollo. Maccabi Healthcare Services, a top Israeli health-care provider in Tel Aviv, is seeking to replicate some Apollo strategies. Then there's Bumrungrad Hospital in exotic Thailand, a luxurious place that claims to have more foreign patients than any other hospital in the world. "It's sort of Ground Zero. I haven't heard anybody yet who's told us that they take more than 350,000 international patients a year," said Curt Schroeder, CEO of Bumrungrad, In a *Sixty Minutes* television interview. "We do have a very unique relationship with Thai Airways," said Schroeder. "So you can buy a ticket. You can use frequent flier mileage to get your checkup. Whatever it takes to get your business."

In conclusion, extreme health care is going to be about the globalization of *world-class* health services. *New York Times* columnist, Paul Krugman, described the American health care problem, "Our system is desperately in need of reform. Yet it will be very hard to get useful reform, for two reasons: vested interests and the privatization ideology of ruling conservatives." So, is there a possible solution even though there is no reform in sight?

While the pharmaceutical and health insurance lobbies in Washington control the policy makers there, business leaders can quietly turn to Dr. Reddy and bring affordable, high-quality health care back to American workers, which are indeed America's greatest business asset. Where there is extreme health care, there's hope for extreme businesses. So, whether it's the Bahamas or Cancun—or specially equipped medical evacuation Airbus A380s for the passage to India— business leaders now have a new world of options for taking on one of the biggest challenges of 21st century business.

TAKEAWAY: A living wage and fundamental benefits such as health care are essential to maintaining any company's chief asset, its people. Companies (especially small businesses) are increasingly being forced to cut or cut back health insurance benefits. But, because the human resource is the most important business resource, going offshore for major levels of health care could soon be an option, promising better quality and far lower costs. While there's a solid business case for business leaders to lead the charge for universal health care, the kind available in Germany, Canada and Japan, smart companies will take matters in their own hands and offshore major healthcare coverage. Health insurance and pharmaceutical companies, watch your backs; you are not immune from globalization, and people are becoming increasingly desperate.

13. Extreme Time.

In his 1988 *Harvard Business Review* article, "Time—The Next Source of Competitive Advantage," George Stalk made an interesting observation about the very nature of competitive advantage: "Like competition itself, competitive advantage is a constantly moving target. For any company in any industry, the key is not to get stuck with a single simple notion of its source of advantage. The best competitors, the most successful ones, know how to keep moving and always stay on the cutting edge. Today, time is on the cutting edge. The ways leading companies manage time—in production, in new product development and introduction, in sales and distribution—represent the most powerful new sources of competitive advantage. Cutting-edge companies today are capitalizing on time as a critical source of competitive advantage: shortening the planning loop in the product development cycle and trimming process time in the factory—managing time the way most companies manage costs, quality or inventory. In fact, as a strategic weapon, time is the equivalent of money, productivity, quality, even innovation. While time is a basic performance variable, management seldom monitors its consumption explicitly—almost never with the same precision accorded to sales and costs. Yet time is a more critical competitive yardstick than traditional financial measures. Time is a fundamental business performance variable."[43]

There are two major aspects of time-based competition,

Response Time (where Lag Time, Lead Time, Inventory Turnover and Cycle Time must be squeezed out in order to meet never-satisfied consumer demands) and *Restructuring Time* (where Reorganization, Asset Reallocation, Business Process Change and Strategy-to-Execution Time are paramount management challenges).

With the advent of the Internet and the New IT (business process management systems), both restructuring and operational response time can be achieved, in large part, virtually.

Focusing on response time, the Spanish superstar, Zara (pronounced Thara), is described by Louis Vuitton fashion director Daniel Piette as, "possibly the most innovative and devastating retailer in the world." Founded two decades ago in a remote, impoverished area of the Iberian peninsula, Zara is to the fashion world what Dell is to the computer world, churning out the latest fashions at budget prices, flipping the fashion industry on its head. In a 2005 press dossier, Zara's parent company states that it has over 2,300 outlets in 56 countries in Europe, The Americas, Asia and Africa, achieving sales in 2004 of over $7 billion, with a net profit of $780 million. In January, 2005 the Group had 47,046 employees.

Using the Internet to speed along customer demand information, Zara can make a completely new design and get it in its boutiques in two weeks, compared to the six to nine month *best practice* in the industry, where traditional retailers outsource most of their production to low-wage countries. Zara, by contrast, makes all but a third of its fashions (see also, the Zara story in *Extreme Supply Chains*). Although percentages vary from season to season, in 2004, 70% of production was carried out in Europe and neighboring countries. A further 27% of total production took place in Asia.

The point of sale at the store is not the end of the process but rather its start. The stores act as market information gathering terminals, providing feedback to the design teams and reporting the trends demanded by customers. Being totally customer focused, stores drive innovation at Zara. Stores electronically send new ideas to headquarters where more than 200 designers analyze designs for merit and then create specifications that are scanned and fed into computer controlled cutting machines to produce the material needed by outside workshops. The high-tech cutting machines are manned by a small number of highly-trained technicians. Zara restocks its stores around the world twice a week, and cranks out 12,000 different designs a year.

The key to this model is the ability to adapt the offer to meet customer desires in the shortest time possible. As stated in its 2005 press dossier, "time is the main factor to be considered, above and beyond production costs." By managing time over cost as the supreme business variable, Zara is able not only to shorten turnaround times, but also achieve greater flexibility, reducing stock to a minimum and diminishing fashion risk to the greatest possible extent. Zara gets it. While other fashion retailers go to Asia and beyond to squeeze out costs, Zara squeezes out costs by squeezing out time.

Time-based competition isn't about the latest gee-whiz technology; it's about a management philosophy that's determined to squeeze out time regardless of the technologies available. Michael Hugos, CIO of at Network Services, a distribution cooperative that sells food-service, specialty papers and janitorial supplies, teaches this lesson by example. "One of our biggest national account customers is a chain of stores that each holiday season uses specially printed paper items to promote its holiday theme. These items are used in the customer's 4,500 stores during November and December, and when January arrives, any remaining inventory has to be written off. The same holiday print designs are never used two years in a row. In years past, there was excess inventory of around four percent, amounting to almost $600,000 in costs that had to be written off by the customer.

"This retail chain hired a new purchasing manager who decided we could all do better than that this holiday season. He announced his intention to reduce excess inventory of the specially printed holiday items by 50 percent or more. We still had to maintain 100 percent product availability for all its stores and minimize expensive movements of inventory from one region to another to meet unexpected demand. Our sales director on the account told me this was a high-visibility project with the customer, and we had to figure out how to do it. He reminded me that it was already halfway through the summer, so we had to be ready to go in 90 days because we would begin stocking inventory in our distribution centers by October. And, of course, we couldn't spend lots of money on this because margins are tight. I experienced a sudden falling sensation in my stomach, and it wasn't due to air turbulence on the flight back from our initial meeting with the retailer."

Hugos turned to Sun Tzu, a Taoist philosopher who lived in China about 2,500 years ago, and who wrote a book, *The Art of War*. Master Sun says, "There are only five notes in the musical scale, but their variations are so many that they cannot all be heard. There are only five basic colors, but their variations are so many that they cannot all be seen." Hugos thought, "Does this mean that there is a combination of basic IT components that I could use to quickly create my end-to-end supply chain picture and keep it constantly updated?"

"What basic IT components do all parties in this supply chain have easy access to, and how can I combine them into the system I need? I'm not going to give you the whole answer because then you wouldn't get to practice your own agility and figure it out for yourself. But I will give you some hints. The components are spreadsheets, text files, e-mail, a few Web pages, a relational database and some Java programs that took about three weeks to write and test."

"We assembled these components into a system that collected data from all members of the supply chain. The data consisted of inventory amounts that were in production, in warehouses and on order. It also included invoice data that showed our deliveries to the customer's stores, which allowed us to track actual demand at the store levels and regional levels. The system was up and running by October. We reduced excess inventory from 4 percent last year to 1.3 percent this year on increased total sales, and the dollar value of the excess inventory dropped to less than $200,000. With what we learned, we will make further improvements and extend the system to cover the rollout of other new products—not just holiday items. Thank you, Master Sun."

The Pace of Innovation. Internet-enabled business process innovations are not one-time events. It's the "pace of innovation" that counts in today's global and often dog-eat-dog business world. Progressive insurance began its journey as a time-based competitor more than a decade ago, when it introduced a fleet of 2,600 "immediate response" vehicles fitted with laptop computers, claims submission software and wireless access to the company's databases. Instead of adjusters responding to claims in seven to 10 days— the standard of the 9-to-5 insurance companies—Progressive was soon completing the process in as few as nine hours.

But Progressive didn't stop there. In 1996, the company gave customers the ability to compare rates online, and a year later to buy policies. In 1998, a new site let customers make payments, track claim status and modify policy information. In 2001, Progressive was the first insurance company to receive wireless payments from customers using Web-enabled personal digital assistants and mobile phones.

By setting the pace of innovation, Progressive grew from a $1.3 billion company in 1991 to a $13.4 billion company in 2004. Just as *price* elasticity measures the limits of customer demand, Progressive learned that *time* elasticity helped it steal customers from slower competitors in what was otherwise a mature market. By saving customers time, Progressive also builds on and reinforces another competitive variable: *trust*, the foundation for building valuable relationships.

TAKEAWAY: The case for "time" as a source of competitive advantage was written way back in 1988 by Boston Consulting Group's George Stalk. Today, it's no longer a management theory, it's a competitive reality. Managing time as a business variable is now as important as managing costs for companies that want to compete and win in the global economy. Time-based competitors set the pace of innovation, provide their customers with rapid response to their needs, and change their business structures as market conditions change. You don't want to compete against time-based competitors; you want to be one.

14. Extreme Change.

Change happens. Nothing in business is more constant or challenging than "change itself," which brings us to the need for radically improving "change management." Although the discipline of change management deals primarily with the human aspects of change, it can be approached from a number of angles and applied to numerous organizational processes. To be effective, change management should be multi-disciplinary, touching all aspects of the organization. However, at its core, change management is primarily a human-centered issue, for it's mainly concerned with how work gets done when change happens. This is because implementing new work processes, technologies, and overcoming resistance to change are fundamentally people issues. But that doesn't mean that psychology and behavior modification are all there is to it; it also means finding new ways to support how humans actually work. Despite advances in business automation over the past fifty years, the heart and soul of every organization is still its people—without whom the organization will stop dead in its tracks. Yet there is presently no complete way to manage the complex, continually changing work processes carried out by humans—and current work support technologies treat people as if they were pinions in a machine. Frankly, we need to do better, and the International Truck and Engine Corporation provides us with an example of how technology-enabled support of change management can provide the foundation for business transformation.

International Truck and Engine Corporation is a wholly owned subsidiary and operating company of Navistar International Corporation. It manufactures medium- to heavy-duty trucks and school buses and accounted for 70% of the parent company's revenues of $9.7 billion in 2004. International has a 40% market share in Class 6-7 medium trucks and maintains its number three position in Class 8 heavy-duty trucks. More children travel to school on International-built school buses than on those of all its competitors combined.

The truck manufacturing industry worldwide is going through the same pattern of stresses and change as did car manufacturing in the 1970s and 1980s: globalization, consolidation, cost slashing, supply chain streamlining, faster product innovation, and, most important of all, a new responsiveness to customers. To complicate matters further the truck market is highly volatile because demand is so dependent on the economy.

There are ten major players in the medium-duty and heavy-duty truck market, all with massive global overcapacity. Most industry commentators expect the industry to be consolidated to no more than five players. Every manufacturer has moved aggressively to cut labor costs, partly through productivity improvements. Renegotiations of union contracts, plant closings and increased rationalization of capacity are the industry norm. So, too, is faster product innovation as the industry responds to increasing customer demands for enhanced features, quality and services.

International Truck and Engine is challenging industry tradition. It is positioning for "exactly in time" manufacturing, with shorter product development cycles, aggressive production cost reduction and freshly designed vehicles built to "car like quality." It aims to cut labor costs per vehicle by 40% and to change the cost dynamics of its business so that it can be profitable on low volume. It has already reduced the number of combinations of engines and transmissions in its medium-duty truck lines from 800 to 34. Its first NGVs (Next Generation Vehicles) were introduced in early 2001, with a continued flow of new models and enhancements coming on a regular schedule.

With this background, International has undertaken a series of innovations in business process management, of which the Product Change Management System (PCMS) initiative is one of the most striking successes.

Time is the issue in all of the sub-processes that make up

International's product development process. Complexity and fragmentation dominated the old process, causing unnecessarily long cycle-times. Producing a truck involves continuous interactions, collaborations and negotiations among multiple parties. Developing new products and enhancing existing ones covers changes to, or new designs of, engines, chassis, mirrors, heating, electronics, seats, axles, fuel fills, gauges, transmissions, controls, welding, fenders, grilles, paint, and many, many other components. These cannot be handled in isolation. Even a small change may affect other areas of design, production and part sourcing. Coordinating changes in the new PCMS involves many departments and external suppliers, and meeting management's demands for collaboration, integration and visibility.

Prior to the PCMS, managers typically had to make a number of phone calls and send several emails in order to verify the status of their change requests. Frequently they would wait for days for a response, often due to key participants being busy, traveling to plants or suppliers, or paper requests being lost or ignored. According to Bill Bailey, Director of Process Development, "In the past, the change management process involved too many 'handoffs' from one group to another. In many instances, engineers under pressures of deadlines and demands from other areas of the business used 'workarounds' (i.e. unauthorized, though understandable, bypassing of the process which was driven by the official request for change). Rework was commonplace when it turned out that some step, or someone, had been left out of the discussions and agreements." International's old product change management process was paper-based and lacked standardization. Members had no clear understanding of the entire process. Critical process information and performance metrics, if they were captured at all, were stored in disparate data repositories and spreadsheets on several hundred desktops and legacy systems. It wasn't uncommon to lose much of this information with employee turnover. Consequently, International suffered unnecessarily long cycle times in an industry where time is of the essence, and represents significant costs.

Senior engineers and marketing professionals spent an inordinate amount of time searching for documents and waiting for approvals. Team members never knew, in real-time, who had committed to deliver a specific element of a product change, who was working on what, and when it was scheduled to be completed. These long cycle times were exacerbated by significant rework and tension among the teams due to lack of clarity and agreement about the work that was to be performed. Process participants had no visibility into the process and they weren't held accountable for their participation. Frequently days would go by before the process owner could get an update as to the status of a change order that was under development. Moreover, International's management was in the dark about a very critical portion of their business, time-to-market.

International's new PCMS resolved all of these issues. International's PCMS is no ordinary kind of technology, for it's not about traditional automation that aims to cut out human work; it's about providing technology support for people-to-people interactions. It can be thought of as a human interaction management system, and is based on Drs. Terry Winograd and Fernando Flores closed-loop business interaction model set forth in their 1983 book, *Understanding Computers and Cognition.*

A common complaint of business people is that technical folks have no real understanding of process. Most technical people view a process as a process map, a set of data systems, and a series of predictable sequential steps. For a business person nothing could be further from the truth. For an executive, a mission-critical process is the sequence of actions that enable the company to deliver on its commitments and add value to customers using a combination of people, methods and tools. Executives, like customers, don't see or care about process maps; they care about customer satisfaction, time-to-market, reduced costs, increased productivity, and improved quality. This lack of understanding frequently makes the step of process redesign a lengthy and frustrating engagement for both technical and business people. So it is only through the use of the human interaction model that process redesign is transformed. As Bill Bailey, head of the Process Development Department, stated, "The interaction model acts as a translator between the language of business and the language of technology."

International's PCMS is a new process design centered on managing and coordinating the negotiations that constitute the process: requests, collaborative agreements and commitments, and approvals. The streamlined process is described in the terms of the "loops" that form the core of the system design and implementation. The PCMS coordinates interactions between an individual or group making a request (the Customer) and the recipient of that request (the Performer) in four phases:

1. Preparation: The Customer proposes work to be done by the Performer and issues a request.
2. Negotiation: The Customer and Performer negotiate until they reach an agreement (commitment) about the work to be fulfilled.
3. Performance: The Performer fulfills the request and

reports completion.

4. Acceptance: The Customer evaluates the work and either declares satisfaction or points out what remains to be done to fulfill the request.

Through the use of the PCMS, the project lead works with his business colleagues to map out the business process by asking questions such as: Exactly what work is required? Who is asking for the work to be performed (i.e. who is in the *role* of the Customer)? Who has to perform the work (i.e. who is in the *role* of Performer)? When is the work due? The model allows business people to assign roles to participants, to create accountability and to eliminate confusion. After a Product Change Request has been approved, a Work Authorization is created. The Product Center Program Manager, acting on behalf of International's end customers, acts as the "Customer" in this sub-process step and requests a change to Engineering. The request is assigned to a Lead Engineer who acts as the "Performer." The two parties negotiate the conditions of satisfaction thereby reducing potential misunderstandings that cause unnecessary delays and rework. Although the Lead Engineer may not actually perform all of the work for the change, accountability remains throughout this entire portion of the process. The Lead Engineer negotiates the actual design and other work with engineers of various skills but all the while maintains the commitment to the "Customer" or Product Center Program Manager. When the product change has been completed, the work is sent back to the *Customer* for approval and acceptance.

A key benefit of using the Model is that no step in a process is considered complete until it is accepted by the *Customer* for that particular step. In other words, a business process designed using the business interaction model becomes a series of loops, representing interactions between parties involved at different stages of the overall process. When a step is done correctly a loop is closed, and the process continues. Using this closed-loop methodology ensures that each step of a job is done accurately and to closure, leading to a desired end-result.

The competitive motivation for the PCMS initiative came from senior management who recognized that efficient planning and integration of product changes could enable the company's business transformation. The product change management process is the most complex of all of International's cross-functional and cross-corporate boundary processes. Successful instances of the process require creativity, collaboration, speed and reliability. It is driven by the Change Request. This is where all the ideas for product change and innovation are created and debated among various department personnel. A Product Center Manager and a Chief Engineer review customer and company needs to determine the potential product changes that will move forward in the process. Overall this sub-process has been reduced from an average of 30 days (in the paper mode) to an average of five days in PCMS (75% reduction). Changes can also now be processed in as little as two days. Senior management summarized the payoffs from its PCMS as: ROI of 362%, 3 month pay back period, increase in productivity of 30% for process chain participants responsible for coordinating and completing key steps of the product change process, cycle time reduction greater than 75%, and reduction in rework along the process chain of steps by 33%.

But, according to Jeff Bauermeister, Process Automation Manager, there is much more to International's process journey. "Our Process Development Team has automated nearly

30 business processes ranging from administrative to key engineering, manufacturing and product development processes. We have taken extreme care to ensure a standard look and feel across all processes. This has resulted in users leveraging their previous Web-based process knowledge, and drastically reduce training time. The training is focused solely on the new process. Another feature is that when you make a process change, it changes all future process instances immediately. Try that with a paper or manual process!"

As in many other areas of manufacturing, the short-term picture in the trucking industry is clouded and discouraging. The long-term scenario is one of increased competition, consolidation, globalization of operations and relationships, and above all, of innovation as the price of staying in business. The new International is innovating everywhere and its new PCMS is at the core of that innovation. For International, the future looks clear and bright, and the lessons learned go beyond its industry; for regardless of the industry, "changing change management" is an imperative for successful 21st century competition.

TAKEAWAY: Change is the only constant in today's business, and change management must be taken to new levels in order to keep pace with the complexity and speed of business. New tools, especially the emerging business process management tools, are needed by companies that want to master change management to compete for the future.

15. Extreme Specialization.

In today's interconnected world, competition in business is increasingly based on supply chains that span companies and continents. The difference between business success and failure is often defined by whose supply chain is more resilient. Add to this mix the ever-present risks to business, both natural and man-made: hurricanes, tsunamis, fires, earthquakes, terrorism, infrastructure accidents, equipment breakdowns, and a host of other calamities, and you have the conditions for a "perfect storm" in the commercial and industrial property insurance industry.

Through super-specialization, one insurance company appears to be thriving under these conditions by helping other businesses weather this perfect storm. Ask anyone at FM Global, a leading insurer of the world's largest companies, and they'll tell you that it is better to prevent a loss than to recover from one. That's the premise upon which FM Global was founded in 1835. The company, which is one of the few mono-line carriers in the insurance industry, continues to operate under that extremely specialized business model today, insuring more than one-third of all Fortune 1000 companies.

What's so specialized about FM Global? It's not bursting at the seams with actuaries. Because the company believes that the majority of all losses are preventable, it does not hire actuaries (whose job is to estimate risk by analyzing statistics). Instead, the company employs more than 1,500 specialized engineers who, backed by advanced scientific research, visit clients' facilities to help assess, prevent, and mitigate risks. This philosophy is based not on theoretical or actuarial risk assumptions, but on more than a century of concrete, scientific research and experience.

Much of FM Global's research and testing takes place at the one-of-a-kind FM Global Research Campus. The work conducted at this $78 million, 1,600-acre facility in West Gloucester, Rhode Island, helps FM Global clients understand how best to prevent significantly physical threats (e.g., fire, natural hazards, electrical equipment breakdown) from affecting their properties and business operations. For example, in the Natural Hazard Laboratory, scientists replicate some of the most severe weather phenomenon, including hurricane-force winds and hailstorms. The tests conducted here help build FM Global's knowledge of what causes building materials to fail and the best ways to design buildings to resist Mother Nature's fury. This knowledge is then passed along to FM Global's clients to help them mitigate or prevent property losses.

FM Global's harnessing of all this engineering knowledge has led to the company's specialization in risk management and property loss prevention. FM Global's in-depth research provides a basis for its cost-effective underwriting solutions and risk assessment services, setting the company apart from its competitors. A perfect example: the 2004 hurricane season. The *Boston Globe* ("Masters of Disaster" article, February 28, 2005) mentions that according to Insurance Information Institute, the four major hurricanes in Florida that year caused estimated losses of more than $21.6 billion. In contrast, FM Global's 1,500 client locations in the state suffered significantly less: only $100 million in total property losses. FM Global provided its Florida accounts with proactive loss prevention engineering services, which helped keep that claim number so relatively low.

In their book, *Blue Ocean Strategy*, W. Chan Kim and Renée Mauborgne wrote, "Cut-throat competition results in nothing but a bloody red ocean of rivals fighting over a shrinking profit pool. Here companies try to outperform their rivals to grab a greater share of existing demand. As the market space gets more and more crowded, prospects for profits and growth are reduced. Products become commodities, and cut-throat competition turns the red ocean bloody. Blue oceans, in contrast, are defined by untapped market space, demand creation, and the opportunity for highly profitable growth. In blue oceans, competition is irrelevant as the rules of the game are waiting to be set."

FM Global, by leveraging its engineering, risk management, and property loss prevention knowledge, appears to have found a "blue ocean" in the commercial and industrial property insurance market. And the move toward more and more multi-company, global supply chains is acting as catalysts for FMGlobal's growth. For FM Global, specialization has been crucial in the company's ascent to its market leadership position. By staying under the radar of its huge competitors in the insurance industry, FM Global has taken such a lead in its engineering versus actuarial insurance business model that it would take competitors five years and major business process disruptions to copy FM Global's business model. During that time, FM Global would capitalize on its lead to move on to yet more innovation.

Super-specialization, where your company is the one and only company that can do what it does, is a vital key to competitive advantage. That is, you want your company to be so specialized that it is a one of a kind, and that the tradeoff costs (financial, brand image, and so on) to copy your unique model would be high enough to be off-putting. Neutrogena soap is an example where its claim to specialization is that it leaves no film on the body. If Dial soap, which is guaranteed to leave an antibacterial film on the body, were to be repositioned against Neutrogena, then all the branding efforts to date for Dial would create conflict in customers' minds. Neutrogena bathes in a Blue Ocean.

As other companies outsource all but their core competencies to specialists, the specialists themselves are exposed to new opportunities. Because the Internet makes it possible to collaborate at the business process level, a superspecialist (be it a country, a community, a company or an individual) can serve a greater number of clients, cutting lead times, lowering costs and enhancing customer service levels with specialized knowledge, capabilities and resources. The superstar teacher in Chennai, India can now sell her services to General Motors, the Chicago public school districts, and the worried parent who wants its child to catch up in his math skills.

Large companies such as Dell, don't tell their specialists scattered across the globe how to do what they do, they simply orchestrate them so that they all add value to Dell's customers. Companies such as Flextronics are in fact superspecialist process orchestrators, calling the tune to multiple subcontractors to design, build and ship products for IBM, HP and others. To be a specialist or to orchestrate specialists, that is the question for 21st century competition.

TAKEAWAY: Now that the world is wired, specialized knowledge plays an even greater role as a business asset. If you have highly specialized knowledge and skills, you now have a worldwide market. On the other hand, your company can now tap superspecialists around the globe, thanks to the universal connectivity of the Internet. The lesson? Be a superspecialist, where you or your company is the one-and-only that can do what you do, and make alliances with other superspecialists that will make your overall value delivery system unstoppable.

16. Extreme Branding.

Today's society is filled with noise. Consumers are hammered with thousands of messages and images each and every day. While brand bullies can spend billions of dollars shouting louder than others, *unbranding* and *no-logo* techniques can be used to earn your name recognition, one customer at a time.

The Luxembourg Internet telephone provider, Skype, doesn't need to advertise, for each customer it gains will want to tell nine others, who, in turn, will want to Skype nine others—pandemic marketing. Since its rollout in 2003, Skype's marketing expenses for advertising and other normal company rollout hoopla is nada, zero. By November 2005, Skype garnered more than 202 million downloads and over 61 million registered users, 3 million-plus of whom are often online concurrently. How were so many Skypers persuaded to sign up? Word of mouth, word of email and blogs.

Meanwhile, in Spain, Zara relies on having prime locations instead of the typical huge advertising budgets of other high-fashion retailers. It spends a meager 0.3% of sales on advertising compared to an average of 3.5% spent by competitors, thanks to its "location, location, location" strategy. It co-locates in high traffic malls and other locations where other retailers' advertising attracts customers to a given location, where customers "discover" the Zara store. Providing "newness" with its "react and respond" business model is what keeps young teens coming back, along with their friends, to see the latest stuff, 17 times a year on average, not just season after season as it is at their competitors' stores—who coincidentally paid for all the advertising that drove traffic to Zara.

The Corporation, both the book by Joel Bakan and the DVD by Mark Achbar, tell a sad story on the state of corporations as exploiters. As consumers revolt over the use of sweatshops, one company has positioned itself to benefit from growing awareness of exploitation to build its brand. While apparel is a universal necessity that transcends almost all cultural and socioeconomic boundaries, most garments are made in exploitative settings. American Apparel has broken this paradigm. It is a manufacturer, distributor and retailer of T-shirts and related products. All of its garments are cut and sewn at its 800,000-square-foot facility in downtown Los Angeles. Every aspect of the production of its garments, from the sewing of the fabric to the photography of the product, is done in-house. By consolidating the entire process, it's able to pursue efficiencies that other companies cannot because of their over reliance on offshore outsourcing. To back up its value of social responsibility, American Apparel, being sweatshop free, offers all of its employees, sewers and administrators alike, basic benefits. The company provides affordable healthcare for workers and their families, company-subsidized lunches, bus passes, free English language classes, on-site masseurs, free parking, proper lighting and ventilation, and the most up-to-date equipment and software.

It offers these as a matter of policy, not only because the company cares about its employees, but also because it understands that a positive work environment is a more productive one. American Apparel is now the largest garment factory in the United States, employing over 3,000 people. American Apparel has 29 retail locations in the United States and 28 international outlets. More stores are opening in 35 cities including Tokyo, Puerto Rico, and Mexico City. While 96% percent of all clothing in the United States is imported (Levi shut its last plants in the U.S. in 2003), American Apparel is the only T-shirt company of its size that does not use offshore labor. Aside from its reputation for being sweatshop free, what makes this company unique is that it has achieved success without having the luxury of a real brand. Visit any Gap store, and you'll find a selection of branded tees. Stop by American Apparel, and there's nary a logo to be found. Some companies have learned that to rise above the noise, silently doing the right thing can create a real buzz.

Marc Gobe, president of a brand-identity consulting firm in New York, told the *Christian Science Monitor*, "People are not buying products today. People are buying emotions. People are buying the value inherent in the brand." But increasingly, branding cannot be achieved with huge ad budgets, for television and radio continue to lose their audiences to TiVo and iPods. TiVo allows viewers to skip through commercials while the iPod lets users listen to hours of music without constantly being interrupted by commercials.

As a result, companies (like the Skype example above) have increasingly turned to viral marketing techniques— techniques that spread like viruses, through word of mouth, e-mail forwards, and Web blogs. This new reality certainly can level the playing field for even the smallest of companies—*if,* and only *if,* they have something *interesting* to communicate. "Advertisers have to find another way to deliver their message," said Peter Sealey, adjunct professor of marketing at the Walter A. Haas School of Business at UC Berkeley. Sealey told the *San Francisco Chronicle*, "Because of the decline in traditional media, they have to make themselves more interesting."[44] The greatest things in branding these days are word-of-mouth, word-of-email, and blogs—but all these require true innovation, not gimmicks, if they are to be mediums carrying your message. In today's world, product innovations such as Skype, or business model innovations such as American Apparel spread like wildfire, no logos required.

Perhaps one of the most dramatic stories of unbranding comes from Holland. Tired of all the commercialization of everything, from the air we breathe to the water we drink? Then just say "No!" At least that's how Neau is pronounced in English. Here's the report from brandchannel.com by Erwin Wijman in Amsterdam, "There is a new brand of water in the Netherlands. Sold as an empty bottle, it requires the buyer to fill up from his own tap. At 100 percent drinking water, Neau is positioning itself explicitly against the bottled mineral water trend.

"In the Netherlands, plain drinking water is of renowned and excellent quality; what's more, it actually tastes good. Holland is one of the few countries in Europe (and in the world) where you can drink water directly from the tap safely, without any health risks. And that is exactly the crux of Neau, says Menno Liauw, of Amsterdam-based advertising bureau Vandejong and Stichting Neau (the Neau Foundation). 'Neau is being sold in empty bottles that you can fill with drinking water, over and over, as often as you like,' he explains. 'Doing this, Neau makes people more aware of the outstanding quality of our day-to-day drinking water to emphasize the contrast with the lousy quality or the total lack of drinkable water in third world countries.'

"The Neau brand has a dual effect: It makes people conscious of the worldwide water problem, and its revenues are spent in drinking water projects in underdeveloped countries in Africa, Vietnam, Peru, and other poor parts of the world. These drinking water projects are being coordinated by well-known Dutch charity organizations like Unicef Nederland and Plan Nederland, with whom Neau cooperates. 'We want to make Neau the conscientious alternative for all those fash-

ionable mineral water brands, like Evian, Viteau and Perrier,'
Liauw says."

Neau is making profits by selling "thin air," but those
profits aren't aimed at the greed of shareholders. They are
aimed at breaking the spell of unbridled branding, and making a small step toward corporations being good citizens as
further discussed in the Strategies section of this book, *Be a
Good Citizen.*

Enough is enough, when it comes to branding. Clean water is clean water, and consumers are tired of Madison Ave-
nue telling them differently. There are lessons here for any
company wanting to genuinely brand its products or services:
e.g., a little straight talk will go a long way, and the word will
spread like wildfire.

TAKEAWAY: Branding used to mean that he who had
the largest advertising and PR budgets created the most noise.
That was yesterday. Today there's simply too much noise for

those ad dollars to overcome, and consumers now have tools such as iPods, Tivo and Web browser pop-up blockers to filter out commercials. New approaches to building name recognition require having a truly unique (versus loud) message, and using word-of-mouth, word-of-email and blogging to spread the word. "No logo" and unbranding philosophies, combined with "viral marketing" techniques, represent new paths forward in branding, and new ways to compete for name recognition. For example, Skype pulled in 61 million registered customers with zero advertising, spreading like wildfire, and earning the individuals who created it billions of dollars with its acquisition by eBay.

Strategies for Extreme Competition.

Recognizing that successful business strategies vary widely from industry to industry, and from company to company, this book makes no foolish attempt to offer cookie-cutter approaches to strategy for your specific company. This book also assumes you are an independent thinker and have significant experience in planning your affairs: you don't need anyone telling you what you must do, or not do. But, with that said, let's recap some of the new realities we've discussed, concentrating our thinking on how strategies might be formulated from them. Let's also contemplate how innovative business ideas that weren't possible before the Internet and the other four drivers of extreme competition are, indeed, posssible now.

Before we begin, let's talk about strategy itself. Three questions to ask yourself in order to see if your company is ready to deal with extreme competition include:

1. Do you have a strategy in place to deal with a market where your product or service is made available for free? In

the U.K., EasyJet is working toward how to stay in business and make money in a world where airline travel is free. In the software market, modeling tool vendors are having to wrestle with the challenges of maintaining revenues when other vendors give away modeling tools. Then again, in software, there's the open-source community, where software and its source code are free. Telecom companies are having to deal with a scenario where Skype means consumers don't pay for phone calls, and everyone is thinking about the day when the Internet is both omnipresent and free—it comes from thin air, perhaps compliments of Google, just like the air that we breathe.

2. Do you know how you will deal with a situation where your competitors can deliver the same goods or service to your clients at the same price (or lower) while operating with overheads that are 20-30% of yours? Internet banks are making inroads into low-operating-cost models. Egg (U.K) has no branch infrastructure to maintain and no ATMs to service, yet still offers the same services as brick and mortar banks.

3. How will you deal with a situation where everyone uses the same technology and business applications as you do? How will you differentiate your company, your products, and your services if your use of IT makes the way you operate a commodity?

The time to put extreme strategies in place is now, because, in the global village, you can be sure that someone is already looking to disrupt your market. Smart companies have their extreme strategies—does yours?

The time to act is now. Centralized, risk-averse organizations will have to overcome entrenched cultures and fiefdoms if they are to become lean and agile innovators. There is no substitute for the very senior-most management teams to restyle their organizations. It's about leadership, leadership and leadership. The corporation as we know it has only been around for a hundred years, and the predominate business models are centered on economies of scale and mass production. With today's realities of globalization and commoditization, alliances and collaboration call for new forms of nimble organizations. This, in turn, requires reshaping the hierarchical and functional management mental models of many incumbent senior executives. Now is the time for companies wanting to thrive in the decade ahead to act on their own creative destruction and reformation.

Be slavishly devoted to your customers. Building loyalty with your present and future customers is the single-most important ingredient for business success in an age where customers have wrested power from suppliers. It's now time to turn your company over to the command and control of your customers, and become their servant, bringing them the very best from the supply side of the supply and demand equation—you'll no longer sell to your customers, you will become their buyers. Your customers don't want just products and services, they want complete solutions that delight.

BPMG founder, Steve Towers, gives some pinpoint advice, "The big question to go and ask the senior people in any organization is: how are you *rewarded* for what you do? The vast majority will have a system whereby rewards are linked to the successful delivery of a range of tasks and activities based on the corporate objectives (inside-out thinking). Until now, this sounded like the right answer, but it's fundamentally flawed. The introduction of successful customer outcomes (outside-in thinking) as a measure of real customer-oriented performance will cut across many of these task-led objectives and, therefore, the reward system. Any company trying to operate like this will never achieve what it is trying to do." Getting closer to your profitable customers means tying your employees' rewards to the right measures, focused upon successful customer outcomes.

Think globally, act globally. With the Internet and jumbo transportation on its side, the smallest of companies, including the sole proprietor, can reach the same markets and the same suppliers that huge transnational corporations reach. Follow John Naisbitt's cue that *the bigger the world economy, the more powerful its smallest players,* and harness the Internet to act globally. That doesn't mean just putting up a Web site. It means using the full range of Internet capabilities so that you and your colleagues, and your information systems and those of your trading partners, collaborate at both the personal level and with your business processes. Reach out and Skype someone. The world's specialists, large and small are now on your desktop.

Be a superspecialist. If you don't want your business to be commoditized, specialize to such a degree that you are the only one that can do what you do—either in absolute terms, or in the local geographic market you serve. Be special, very special. How do you do that? As an individual or a company, finding the "new jobs that need doing" is the key. When this author wrote his first computer program by wiring control boards, the terms programmer or systems analyst didn't exist as job categories. Today we not only have those jobs, we have database analysts, Web programmers, and digital artists. A full array of new jobs that need doing will emerge now that the world has three billion new capitalists pushing innovation. But these new jobs won't be based in yesterday's skills. They will belong to the superspecialists with up-to-the-minute specialized knowledge and skills.

Connect with the superspecialists. There are two basic ways to address the problem of your offerings becoming fungible: build a specialization that is unique in the world and market your specialty to the entire world, or bring your or your affiliates' specialized offerings to a geographic market, where on-site delivery cannot be substituted. Ideo, the world-class design firm, does the former, Tampa's new digital heart hospital does the latter. Britney Spears does the former, this author's plumber who dropped by to fix a leaky faucet last week does the latter. Then again, there's a mix between the two, where the heart surgeon uses a radiologist in Chennai to analyze X-rays taken in Chicago. Outsource, insource, homesource, ruralsouce—do whatever it takes to bring the most compelling value to your most valued customers.

Be a brand master, fight brand bullies. The Internet, TiVo and the iPod have special techniques designed to cut out ads. Theses new technologies have splintered traditional mass media such as radio and television that once served as the cornerstone of branding. Now, companies must target specific customers by using the right medium for the message. The new holy grail is to introduce unique experiences that will spread like wildfire via word-of-mouth, and word-of-email and blogs (e.g., Skype). Whether its through interactive Web sites or other means, companies must become more engaging, more innovative, not more pushy with ads that simply get drowned out by all the noise.

Lands End's "My Personal Model" offers an interactive shopping experience where the customer supplies information about his or her hair color, height, shoulders, hips, waist, and waist placement. Then clothes are checked out to a digital dressing room where they can be tried on the model. "Window shopping" will never be the same, and those who have used the interactive system tell others, even though they did nothing more than window shop. For Lands End, such viral marketing is an ad-free means of branding. Traditional mass media advertising should now be the last option—quit beating your customers over the head with ads. Now is the time to respect your customers, and offer unbranded, logo-free products (American Apparel) and let your customers, who are sick of being bombarded with advertising, spread the word. It's not "advertising as usual" that will create great 21st century brands. But then, in the 21st century, it's not "business as usual."

Embrace time-based competition. Squeezing out time means squeezing out the right kinds of costs. Dump those warehouses full of inventory in favor of just-in-time inventories delivered based on demand, not based on forecast. Forecasts are, by definition, wrong; and in 21st century markets, a business cannot afford to be wrong. Time-based competition, doesn't mean buying zillion-dollar real-time technology and systems. Time-based competition is a management approach that aims to squeeze out time, regardless of the technical means employed. It often means using what's already available, the Internet and common tools such as spread sheets and email alerts, to radically improve your cycle times.

To embrace time-based competition, a company needs strategies to become, what may best be called, a *real-time enterprise*. The goal is to position the company between its customers and the global sources of supply that can be tapped to meet customers' needs *when* and *where* they want those ever-changing needs met—and that usually means *now*. Getting between customers and suppliers doesn't mean creating an impedance mismatch between suppliers and customers. It means becoming an amplifier whose volume controls are operated by the customer.

Grok process! Science fiction writer Robert Heinlein, in his novel *Stranger in a Strange Land*, used the word "grok" as part of the fictional Martian language. In the Martian tongue, as described by a character in the novel, "*Grok* means to understand so thoroughly that the observer becomes a part of the observed—to merge, blend, lose identity in group experience." The book, *Business Process Management: The Third Wave*, heralds *process* as "the breakthrough that redefines competitive advantage for the next fifty years." It was the mastery of process that propelled Japan from maker of junk toys to the gold standard in quality. Now, with the ubiquitous connectivity of the Internet, the capability of process management must be used to squeeze out friction and costs, and to deploy supra-business processes that simply weren't possible before.

And it's not enough to just build an outstanding end-to-end business process crossing suppliers and customers. That process must be "built to change," for change is the only certainty. Business process management tools with "change built in" are now readily available for even the smallest of companies—they are becoming as universally available as email. However, the process tools alone, like all tools, won't make you a process-managed company; but becoming a process-managed company requires the use of appropriate 21st century tools. The task is to change the thinking in your company from functional management to process management, and get the right tools to do the job.

Embrace the New IT. Although the new category of business software, the New IT, called business process management, completely changes the way companies use technology for competitive advantage, the message hasn't yet reached the executives in the corner offices in most companies. BPM isn't about automating recordkeeping, it's about a fresh new technology-enabled capability for operational innovation. As long-time business process practitioner and chairman of the Dutch BPM Forum, Frits Bussemaker, explains, "Even though many internal BPM practitioners have identified substantial business benefits from the use of an automated BPM solution, they have often struggled to convince the rest of the organization, especially the decision makers and holders of the budgets, to gain funding."

BPM isn't just another IT tool for IT people, it's the breakthrough that gives business people what they have wanted all along—the capability to manage their business processes directly without the requirement of changing hard-wired business systems for every new or changed business process. Thus, it's senior executives, in large and small companies alike, that must come to recognize this new business capability, and ensure that it becomes part of the company's competitive arsenal. Bussemaker makes it clear, "it is crucial to focus on the business benefits, rather than technology." Spend time learning about business process management, educate your top managers, experiment with and then select the right tools, and start your journey to becoming a process-managed enterprise.

Offer process-powered self-service. Today's customers will no longer tolerate touch-tone hell and run the gauntlet at call centers to get what they want. Why put some keyboard operator, also known as a call-center representative, in between customers and the information and services they need? Process-powered self-service technologies are now readily available that allow your customers to explore on their own, select on their own, and troubleshoot on their own. But process-powered self-service doesn't mean that a customer is to be left alone without additional support. In some cases, a solution to a customer's problem is not immediately available. But today's self-service capabilities also provide a collaboration environment so that customers can have a *dialog* with a company to solve issues that were not anticipated and not built into predefined self-service techniques. As Pehong Chen pointed out earlier in this book, "In a high-touch self-service model, customers retain visibility into the process and remain a participant—receiving alerts and notifications at points in the process that require input, decisions or collaboration with others involved in the process. All participants have visibility into status, action items and previous activity relating to the process. Rule-driven aspects of the process move forward without requiring an intermediary." As a business strategy, embracing process-powered self-service provides double leverage: cutting costs and providing better levels of service.

Offer product-services and experiences. As GE's CEO, Jeff Immelt, told an audience at Cornell University, "Unless you can differentiate yourself, unless you can present yourself to customers, you can't make margins and you can't make money." Then, turning to Pine and Gilmore's business model for the experience economy, a company must know where it stands on a spectrum from commodity, to goods, to services to experiences. Just as GE progressed from being a products company to a services company that also offers great products, any company must develop strategies to climb the food chain and offer compelling experiences to the customers they want to keep. While that doesn't mean dancing for your dinner, it does mean offering total solutions. It also means supporting your customers throughout the purchase and consumption of your goods and services—your customers don't want a drill, they want a hole; your customers don't want a kitchen cabinet, they want a happy kitchen. And your customers' needs will change as they change—a year or so after your customer's wedding it just may be time to help them with the goods and services they'll need with that first baby. In all these cases, as well as others, your customers want the emotional satisfaction that comes with complete and positive experiences. Do all you can to provide the experiences that your customers really want. Climb Pine and Gilmore's food chain, for that's what it now takes to succeed.

Systematize innovation. The price of success is follow-on failure if you cling to that success. Any sufficiently innovative product or service will be the target of all your competitors, near and far. If indeed it's innovation that's the secret sauce of business success in the 21st century, then it's got to be "the pace of innovation" and not the innovation itself that sustains competitive advantage. With three billion new capitalists breathing down your neck, you must have a systematic approach to business innovation that is capable of heading out for the next innovation after any given innovation. To set the pace of innovation in your industry, all the dimensions of business innovation (Operational, Organizational, Supply-side, Core-competency, Sell-side, and Product & Service innovation) must be considered in order to become a serial innovator. Innovation isn't an event or a single product invention, it's the approach to problem solving discussed in *Innovating Innovation* that counts, and that approach must account for all dimensions of business innovation. Make innovation a systematic, repeatable business process in order to win in the brave new world of competition. How many identifiable innovation projects do you have in your company, right now? Have you formed teams for innovation or appointed individuals to the task? Do you measure success of your innovation efforts across all six dimensions of business innovation?

Be a good citizen. Right now, it's tough to see that America has a strategy for globalization and extreme competition. If America continues to drive its economy simply by its citizens buying (flipping) each others houses, it will end up on the zero side of a zero sum game—undereducated, underskilled, uninsured, overspent, non-savers won't inherit the wealth of the 21st century. As individuals, Americans must stop the pattern of consumption, consumption and more consumption—the buy now, pay later party won't last.

Sometimes, success can only be achieved if it is nurtured. Instead of continuing slash-government-to-the-bone budget cuts, now is the time for the American government to invest more in education, in research, in infrastructure renovation, in science, and in technology in order to maintain the country's leading edge. Who is going to deliver the 250 mpg car if government won't nurture it. Who is pushing for a "Manhattan project" to make that happen? Don't the powerbrokers in Washington see the perfect storm in energy as China presses on with its industrialization and its people switch from bicycles to cars? Business leaders must demand more support from government on these issues if they want their nation to remain competitive. This discussion isn't a left-wing tax and spend discussion, it's an appeal to business leaders that want to be competitive in the global markets of the 21st century, with three billion new capitalists who are backed by serious investments from their governments.

It's also time to reverse the trend where small businesses are forced to opt out of providing their employees with health care to reconsider the competitive advantage of universal health care, so Toyota or others won't go to Canada where employees do have universal health care. As subtitled in the book, *The Corporation,* "The Pathological Pursuit of Profit and Power," simply cannot be a sustained source of competitive advantage. In 1886, a Supreme Court decision gave corporations the status of "persons" under the law (a law originally intended for freed black slaves!), granting them the protections of the 14th Amendment to the Constitution. Today, corporations have the same legal status as "persons," but without the legal or moral obligation to the welfare of workers, the environment, or the well-being of society as a whole—by law, they answer only to stockholders, who, in turn, want short-term profits.

If you as a corporation want to be that legal entity of "person," then you as a corporation have an ethical mandate to go beyond the pathological pursuit of profit and power to improve the society you as a "person" live in. The world has had enough of the Enrons, and it's now time to understand that treating other persons as you, as a corporate "person," would like to be treated, has come.

Don't fool people that your diet sweetener is simply made from sugar, when, as you can read at Wikipedia.com, it's actually a chlorinated disaccharide. Chlorinated compounds (such as DDT and other pesticides) may be stored in body fat, and the FDA determined that up to about 27% of sucralose can be absorbed by the body. In a response to a request by the FDA for comments on a proposed monograph for sucralose for inclusion in the Food Chemicals Codex, Malkin Solicitors stated that the name sucralose is inaccurate, deceptive, and will mislead consumers because of the close similarity to the name sucrose, a product for which sucralose might be a replacement. Because sucralose is a chlorinated version of a disaccharide, Malkin contended that the common name should not misrepresent the makeup of the material.

Malkin contended that the common name should indicate that the material is a chlorinated disaccharide, reflect the presence of chlorine, and avoid confusion with sucrose. Malkin stated that the name used by the FAO/WHO JEFCA "trichlorogalactosucrose" or a similarly accurate name such as trichlorofructogalactose should be used. FDA lobbyists aside, it's time to provide complete information to customers, if for no other reason than they now have increased powers to find more complete information from each other (just search sucralose at Wikipedia.com where the above information was derived). In short, customers can now create their own information realities by sharing information in ways never before possible.

This book isn't making conclusions about the safety of products or proffering a treatise on politics. It's just making the point that good citizenry is now a major business variable. With the power of information in the hands or the ordinary man, thanks to the Internet, a more complete truthfulness is now a competitive advantage. That wasn't always so during the rise of the Industrial Age, but it is now, especially with the growing demand for *green products*. The CIO of a $7 billion distributor of maintenance supplies, industrial packaging, and food service disposables told this author that, in the summer of 2005, green products were all the talk in his industry. The industry now knows it must respond anew to a fully informed customer that wants to know what's really in stuff, and leaders in that industry know that they must start putting "green" into their stuff, or be left behind in a toxic dump.

Do the right thing, not only because it's the right thing, but also because fully informed customers are mad as hell and won't take anything less that the whole truth anymore. It's time for all "persons" (that also includes corporations according to the Supreme Court in America) to become good citizens: let no corporation be left behind.

Strategy Recap. As we mentioned in the opening of this book, it can be useful to turn our attention to Joseph Schumpeter's ideas of "creative destruction" as the engine of the renovation. This is from the *Concise Encyclopedia of Economics:* *"Capitalism, Socialism, and Democracy* was much more than a prognosis of capitalism's future. It was also a sparkling defense of capitalism on the grounds that capitalism sparked entrepreneurship. Indeed, Schumpeter was among the first to lay out a clear concept of entrepreneurship. He distinguished inventions from the entrepreneur's innovations. Schumpeter pointed out that entrepreneurs innovate, not just by figuring out how to use inventions, but also by introducing new means of production, new products, and new forms of organization. These innovations, he argued, take just as much skill and daring as does the process of invention.

"Innovation by the entrepreneur, argued Schumpeter, led to gales of "creative destruction" as innovations caused old inventories, ideas, technologies, skills, and equipment to become obsolete. The question, as Schumpeter saw it, was not 'how capitalism administers existing structures,... [but] how it creates and destroys them.' This creative destruction, he believed, caused continuous progress and improved standards of living for everyone.

"Schumpeter argued with the prevailing view that 'perfect' competition was the way to maximize economic well-being. Under perfect competition all firms in an industry produced the same good, sold it for the same price, and had access to the same technology. Schumpeter saw this kind of competition as relatively unimportant. He wrote: '[What counts is] competition from the new commodity, the new technology, the new source of supply, the new type of organization... competition which... strikes not at the margins of the profits and the outputs of the existing firms but at their foundations and their very lives.'"

The future is not some manifest destination; it's our own creation, perhaps most often through our own creative destruction. The paths to it are not discovered, they are forged, and the process changes both the path maker and the destination. There are no cookie-cutter approaches to getting your particular company ready for extreme competition, and it isn't an event; it's a way of business. Most of all, it's your mission, should you choose to accept that *your* future is in *your* hands.

Grand notions of business change are particularly problematic. It all boils down to "what should you do next Monday morning?" While there are no secret formulas, business leaders are well advised to evaluate the sixteen new realities of 21st century business, and ponder business innovations that were once thought to be impractical prior to the wiring of the planet; the resources embodied in three billion new capitalists; the New IT; and the advent of jumbo transportation.

Rather than ripping your company apart, innovative business strategies can now be embraced *incrementally* with technology enablement—one breakout strategy at a time. Change in strategy and operational transformations become matters of portfolio management, not big-bang, rip and replace disruptions. There is much to learn, and many cultural barriers to overcome, but Monday morning is a good day to start your company's incremental business reformation. Better still, *today* is a great day to start your company's journey to becoming an extreme competitor.

References

1 Schumpeter uses "creative destruction" as a phrase in which old ways of doing things are endogenously destroyed and replaced by the new. Schumpeter thinks that the success of capitalism will lead to a form of corporation and a fostering of values, especially among intellectuals, of hostility to capitalism. The intellectual and social climate needed to allow entrepreneurship to thrive will not exist in advanced capitalism and it will be succeeded by socialism of some form or another. There will not be a revolution, but merely a trend in parliaments to elect social democratic parties of one stripe or another. Schumpeter emphasizes that he is analyzing trends, not engaging in political advocacy.

2 *Drucker, Peter, "Survey: The Near Future,"* The Economist, November 2, 2001.

3 http://www.financetech.com/featured/showArticle.jhtml? articleID=14701418

4 http://www.chiefexecutive.net/depts/technology/197a.htm

5 *http://www.nwlink.com/~donclark/history_knowledge/ mcluhan.html*

6 *Peter Drucker, "Beyond the Information Revolution,"* Atlantic Monthly, October 1999.

7 Ajax is an acronym for Asynchronous JavaScript and XML

8 *Dennis H. Jones, "The New Logistics,"* in Blueprint to the Digital Economy, McGraw Hill, 1998.

9 Cargo Statistics, U.S. Commercial Air Carriers, *Fiscal Years 1970–2002, Federal Aviation Administration, Office of Aviation Policy & Plans.*

10 ttp://www.fedex.com/us/about/news/speeches/europe.html

11 http://www.business2.com/b2/web/articles/1,17863,655497,00.html

12 http://www.nytimes.com/2005/08/29/opinion/29 krugman.html

13 Globalization's Next Victim: US, Production, wealth, power, services and technology are slip-sliding away to the East, Clyde Prestowitz, San Francisco Chronicle, July 10, 2005.

14 *Drucker, Peter, "Survey: The Near Future,"* The Economist, November 2, 2001.

15 Informating is a term coined by Shoshonna Zuboff of the Harvard Business School in her book, *In the Age of the Smart Machine: The Future of Work and Power* (1990). Zuboff has observed how information and communication technologies have created an almost magical "looking

glass" into an organization's core.

[16] Joe Giffler, "Capturing Customers For Life," *Decision Magazine,* May 1998.

[17] Reichfield and Sasser Harvard Business Review 1990.

[18] Michael Meltzer, NCR Corporation, "Using the Data Warehouse to Drive Customer Retention, Development and Profit," http://www.crm-forum.com/crm_forum_white_papers/crpr/ppr.htm

[19] Kevin Kelly, *New Rules for the New Economy: 10 Radical Strategies for a Connected World,* Viking Press, November, 1998.

[20] http://www.centrobe.com/news/keynotes/neosphere98.asp

[21] Paul McNabb and Mike Steinbaum, "Reclaiming Customer Care: The Milkman Returns," Cambridge Information Network, 1999.

[22] Rich Melmon, Partner, The McKenna Group, "Real-time Marketing versus One-to-One Marketing," http://www.mckenna-group.com/realtime/rt/index.html

[23] http://www.bpmg.org/articles.php

[24] Don W. Caudy, "Using R&D Outsourcing as a Competitive Tool," *Medical Device & Diagnostic Industry Magazine,* March, 2001.

[25] Don W. Caudy, "Using R&D Outsourcing as a Competitive Tool," *Medical Device & Diagnostic Industry Magazine,* March, 2001

[26] Christopher Koch, "Innovation Ships Out," *CIO Magazine,* January 2005.

[27] http://www.businessweek.com/magazine/content/03_41/b3853096_mz017.htm

[28] Chairman Jack Welch's remarks at the firm's annual shareowners meeting in Atlanta, GA, April 25, 2001.

[29] References for Extreme Customization:

1) The Customer Centric Enterprise. Advances in Mass Customization and Personalization by Mitchell M. Tseng (Editor), Frank T. Piller (Editor)

2) BusinessWeek , April 18 2005

3) Business 2.0,January/February 2005

4) http://www.norwichunion.com/info/pay-as-you-drive.htm

5) http://www.stylingcard-ag.com/pages/index.cfm?dom=2 StylingCard

[30] References for Avendra:

1) http://www.nola.com/business/t-p/index.ssf?/base/money-

2/1109860982101481.xml

2) http://www.businessweek.com/technology/content/
oct2004/tc20041029_9592_tc024.htm

3) http://www.ipodlounge.com/

4) http://www.forbes.com/personaltech/2004/11/18/
cx_ld_1118ipod.html

5) http://www.avendra.com/

6) http://www.outsourcing-center.com/

References For Flextronics

1) http://www.itweb.co.za/office/flextronics/ pressclipping2.htm

2) www.flextronics.com

3) http://www.businessworldindia.com/june2104/ news09.asp

4) Business Week – March 21 2005

5) http://www.time.com/time/global/august/cover.html

6) http://www.purchasing.com/article/CA237778.html

31 From: Bill Gates | Sent: Thu May 19 10:55:42 2005 | To: (Microsoft customers) | Subject: The New World of Work

32 Deborah Asbrand, "Squeeze out excess costs with supply-chain solutions," *Datamation,* March, 1997.
http://www.datamation.com/PlugIn/issues/1997/march/03mfg.html

33 David Truog, "The End Of Commerce Servers," *The Forrester Report.* March 1999.

34 Deborah Asbrand, "Squeeze out excess costs with supply-chain solutions," *Datamation,* March, 1997.
http://www.datamation.com/PlugIn/issues/1997/march/03mfg.html

35 June Langhoff, "Chain of Command: Forging New Partnerships, Building Bigger Profit Margins," Oracle Magazine, *Profit,* November, 1997.
http://www.oramag.com/profit/97-Nov/chain.html

36 Mathew Schwartz, "Extending the Supply Chain," *Software Magazine,* November, 1998. http:www.softwaremag.com/Nov98/sm118eb.htm

37 David L. Anderson, Frank E. Britt, and Donavon J. Favre, "The Seven Principles of Supply Chain Management," *Logistics Online,* 1997.
http://www.manufacturing.net/magazine/logistic/archives/1997/scm r/11princ.htm

38 Jonathan Byrnes, You Only Have One Supply Chain? Harvard Business School, Working Knowledge, Auguat, 2005.

39 *John Schmid, "China engineers its next great leap,"* Milwaukee Journal Sentinel, Dec. 30, 2003.

[40] http://economictimes.indiatimes.com/ articleshow/msid-1174800, curpg-1.cms

[41] http://www.sfgate.com/cgi-bin/article.cgi?file=/c/a/2005/07/10/INGRADJF3K1.DTL

[42] "US science may be in crisis," *New Scientist,* October 2005.

[43] Stalk, George, "Time—The Next Source of Competitive Advantage," *Harvard Business Review,* July-August, 1988.

[44] http://www.sfgate.com/cgi-bin/article.cgi?file=/chronicle/ ar-chive/2005/08/27/BUGEQEE3LH1.DTL&type =business

Extreme Readings

Bhagwati, Jagdish, *In Defense of Globalization,* Oxford University Press, 2004.

Bono, Edward de, *Six Thinking Hats,* Penguin Books, 1999.

Business Process Management Group, *In Search Of BPM Excellence: Straight From The Thought Leaders,* Meghan-Kiffer Press, 2005.

Carayol, Rene and Firth, David, *Corporate Voodoo—Principles for Business Mavericks and Magicians,* Capstone, 2001.

Chesbrough, Henry, *Open Innovation—The New Imperative for Creating and Profiting from Technology,* Harvard Business School Press, 2003.

Chowdhury, Subir, *Design For Six Sigma—The Revolutionary Process for achieving Extraordinary Profits,* FT Prentice Hall, 2003.

Christensen, Clayton, Scott D., Anthony, Roth A., Erik, *Seeing What's Next—Using the Theories of Innovation to Predict Industry Change,* Harvard Business School Press, 2004.

Christensen, Clayton M., *The Innovator's Solution—Creating and Sustaining Successful Growth,* Harvard Business School Press, 2003.

Davenport, Thomas H. and Laurence Prusak, *Working Knowledge,* Harvard Business School Press, 2000.

Davenport, Thomas H., *Thinking for a Living: How to Get Better*

Performance And Results from Knowledge Workers, Harvard Business School Press, 2005.

*** Fingar, Peter, and Joseph Bellini, *The Real-Time Enterprise: Competing on Time,* Meghan-Kiffer Press, 2005.

Fingar, Peter, and Ronald Aronica, *The Death of "e" and the Birth of the Real New Economy: Business Models, Technologies and Strategies for the 21st Century,* Meghan-Kiffer Press, 2005.

** Foster, Richard, and Sarah Kaplan, *Creative Destruction: Why Companies That Are Built to Last Underperform the Market--And How to Successfully Transform Them,* Currency, 2001.

Goldratt, Eliyahu M. and Cox, Jeff, *The Goal* (2nd Ed.), Gower, 1993.

Graham, Douglas and Bachmann, Thomas T., *Ideation—The Birth and Death of Ideas,* Wiley, 2004.

Hargagon, Andrew, *How Breakthroughs Happen—The Surprising Truth About How Companies Innovate,* Harvard Business School Press, 2003.

** Harrison-Broninski, Keith, *Human Interactions: The Heart And Soul Of Business Process Management: How People Really Work And How They Can Be Helped To Work Better,* Meghan-Kiffer Press, 2005.

Jones, Tim, *Innovating At The Edge—How Organizations Evolve and Embed Innovation Capability,* Butterworth Heinemann, 2002.

** Kaplan S., Robert, Norton P., David, *Strategy Maps—Converting Intangible Assets Into Tangible Outcomes,* Harvard Business School Press, 2004.

Kelley, Tom and Littman, Jonathan, *The Art of Innovation— Lessons in Creativity from IDEO, America's Leading Design Firm,* Profile Books, 2004.

Khan, Rashid N., *Business Process Management: A Practical Guide,* Meghan-Kiffer Press, 2005.

Kim, W. Chan, and Renée Mauborgne, *Blue Ocean Strategy: How to Create Uncontested Market Space and Make Competition Irrelevant,* Harvard Business School Press, 2005.

Klein, Naomi, *No Logo: Taking Aim at the Brand Bullies,* Picador, 2000.

Managing Creativity and Innovation, Harvard Business Essentials, Harvard Business School Press, 2003.

McConnell, Carmel, *Change Activist—Make Big Things Happen Fast,* Pearson Education, 2003.

Miller, William L. and Morris, Langdon, *Fourth Generation R&D—Managing Knowledge, Technology and Innovation,* Wiley, 1999.

Myerson, Jeremy, *IDEO: Masters of Innovation,* Lawrence King Publishing, 2001.

Ould, Martyn A., *Business Process Management: A Rigorous Approach,* Meghan-Kiffer Press, 2005.

** Pine, Joseph, and James H. Gilmore, *The Experience Economy: Work Is Theatre & Every Business a Stage*, Harvard Business School Press, 1999.

** Prestowitz, Clyde, *Three Billion New Capitalists,* Basic Books,

2005.

Ridderstråle, Jonas and Nordström, Kjelle, *Funky Business—Talent Makes Capital Dance,* Pearson Education Limited, 2002.

Schrage, Michael, *Serious Play—How the world's best companies simulate to innovate,* Harvard Business School Press, 2000.

Schumpeter, Joseph A., *Capitalism, Socialism, and Democracy,* Harper Perennial, 1962.

Senge, Peter, *The Dance of Change—The Challenging to Sustaining Momentum in Learning Organizations,* Currency Doubleday, 1999.

** Senge Peter, *The Fifth Discipline—The Art & Practice of the Learning Organization,* Randomhouse, 1990.

*** Smith, Howard and Fingar, Peter, *Business Process Management: The Third Wave,* Meghan-Kiffer Press, 2003.

** Smith, Howard and Fingar, Peter, *IT Doesn't Matter—Business Processes Do,* Meghan-Kiffer Press, 2003.

** Spanyi, Andrew, *Business Process Management is a Team Sport: Play it to Win!* Meghan-Kiffer Press, 2004.

Stiglitz, Joseph E., *Globalization and Its Discontents,* W. W. Norton & Company, 2003.

Zyman, Sergio with Brott, Armin A., *Renovate Before You Innovate—Why Doing the New Thing may not be the Right Thing,* Portfolio, 2004.

Index

About the Author and Contributors

Peter Fingar, Executive Partner in the business strategy firm, Greystone Group, is one of the industry's noted experts on business process management, and a practitioner with over thirty years of hands-on experience at the intersection of business and technology. Equally comfortable in the boardroom, the computer room or the classroom, Peter has taught graduate computing studies in the U.S. and abroad. He has held management, technical and advisory positions with GTE Data Services, American Software and Computer Services, Saudi Aramco, EC Cubed, the Technical Resource Connection division of Perot Systems and IBM Global Services. He developed technology transition plans for clients served by these companies, including GE, American Express, MasterCard and American Airlines-Sabre. In addition to numerous articles and professional papers, he is an author of six best-selling books. Peter has delivered keynote talks and papers to professional conferences in America, Austria, Australia, Canada, South Africa, Japan, United Arab Emirates, Saudi Arabia, Egypt, Bahrain, Germany, Britain, Italy and France.

Sandeep Arora is the author of *Business Process Management. Process is the Enterprise.* Sandeep graduated from the Indian Institute of Technology in Kharagpur. Arora currently works as Tech Lead for BPM systems at FM Global in Johnston, RI. In the past he has worked as a consultant with Lockheed Martin, AMS, Pitney Bowes, Swiss Bank (now UBS) and Avon Products. Arora's writings can be found at bpm-strategy.com

Sue Bushell is Contributing Editor for *CIO Magazine* in Sydney, Australia, and an Independent Writer assisting high-tech companies in communicating complex ideas in clearly understandable business terms. sbushell@bigpond.net.au

Hitoshi Shirai is an author of best-selling books on e-government, e-commerce and related IT areas, Deputy Director of the Hitachi Research Institute in Tokyo, and HRI's Chief Researcher for the Japanese Government's efforts to make Japan the "World's Most Advanced IT Nation."

Abhinandhan Prateek is a Computer Science graduate of the Indian Institute of Technology in Bombay. After serving in posts with Tata Consultancy Services, Netscape and Oracle he founded Agneya Infotech, headquartered in Hyderabad.

Mark McGregor is Director and Chief Coach of the BPM Group, a non-profit organization dedicated to furthering the aims and objectives of individuals and organisations in the Business Process Management field. His major writings appear at BPMG.org.

Omar Mark Ragel, a 30-year IT veteran in the Middle East, is Managing Director of BPM-Middle East, with offices and operations throughout the Gulf Cooperation Council (GCC) countries (Bahrain, Kuwait, Oman, Qatar, Saudi Arabia and the United Arab Emirates). Ragel's process initiatives are described at www.bpm-me.com

Frits Bussemaker is the founder and chairman of the BPM-Forum, a non-profit organization serving business process management professionals in the Netherlands and Belgium. Visit www.bpm-forum.org for more information. He has worked in the IT industry since the 1980s and is a regular speaker at conferences on business process management.

Steve Towers is the co-founder and CEO of the non-profit Business Process Management Group, a global business club exchanging ideas and best practice in BPM and change management. BPMG.org has over 14,000 members across all continents.

Shridhar Rangarajan graduated with a BSc in Physics and MSc in Computer Science from the University of Poona in Pune, India. He is a Senior Architect at Herzum Software, an international consulting company specializing in IT strategy and enterprise architecture, headquartered in Chicago, Il. Previously, he served as Senior Software Consultant at Patni Computer Systems in Mumbai, India, and Lead Software Engineer for a major e-business startup in Connecticut.

Jesse Shiah is a Computer Engineering graduate of the Taipei Institute of Technology in Taiwan and also received both Computer and MBA degrees from University of Massachusetts at Amherst. He has served in engineering and management positions with the DataViews division of Dynatech (acquired by GE), Uniscape, and a crack engineering team at Trados, serving Global 2000 companies, including Hewlett-Packard and Nokia. Shiah co-founded Ascentn, a high-tech business process management company headquartered in Mountain View, CA.

Gene Weng graduated from the University of Science and Technology of China in Beijing with a MS in Mathematics, and from the University of Oregon with a MS in Computer Science. He taught at the Beijing Information Technology Institute. Previously, he was an IT Architect at Perot Systems, and currently holds the same position in the Automated Decisioning group of Wells Fargo.

Jae-Hyoung Yoo is a graduate of Yonsei University in Seoul with BS and MS degrees in Electronics Engineering and a PhD degree in Computer Engineering. Mr. Yoo joined KT (formerly Korea Telecom) Research Center in 1986 and has led various initiatives in the development of Network Management Systems. He is currently an assistant Vice President at KT overseeing the development of the next generation network operations support systems.

Chee-Seng Low is an Engineering graduate of the National University of Singapore and received a MBA degree from Nanyang Technological University. After serving at various senior management positions in Nortel, Telecom Equipment (a subsidiary of SingTel, formerly Singapore Telecom) and Star-Hub, he founded Eminuum, headquartered in Singapore.

Charles Koh earned his MBA from New York University, MS in Computer Science at the Pratt Institute, and BA in Mathematics from the University of Hawaii. Born in Korea, he is President of Millenium Infosystems, and previously held technical, management, and consulting posts with NASA, the Federal Reserve Bank of New York, the Imperial Iranian Air Force, General Electric, and Arthur Young (Ernst and Young).

Companion Book …
An in-depth analysis of time-based competition.

Time is the scarcest resource. —Peter Drucker

The REAL-TIME ENTERPRISE

Competing on Time with the Revolutionary Business SEx Machine

PETER FINGAR
JOSEPH BELLINI
Foreword by Dr. Max More

The Definitive Guides to the New IT.